NEW YORK TIMES B

A CREATIVE REBEL'S GUIDE TO

WRITING AMAZING FICTION

MEGHAN MARCH

ISBN-13: 978-1-943796-56-4

A Creative Rebel's Guide to Writing Amazing Fiction

Meghan March

The Creative Rebel Company

CONTENTS

PART THREE
THE REST OF THE PROCESS

ABOUT *A CREATIVE REBLE'S GUIDE TO WRITING AMAZING FICTION*

Creative flow has blessed me with 39 novels that have collectively sold over five million copies, in 16 languages, in under eight years, earning me over $10 million and over 50 spots on the *New York Times*, *Wall Street Journal*, *USA Today*, and foreign bestseller lists.

All my dreams came true because I learned to write amazing fiction.

I wrote this book for the old me. The girl who had big dreams, but no real idea how to write the books she'd need to make those big dreams come true. I wanted to make it easier for her to get to where I am now by sharing what I learned along the way. I wanted her to be able to leap over the pitfalls where I stumbled, avoid the challenges that held me back, and glide past the emotional despair, mental anguish, and burnout I faced.

I wrote this book because my readers said that no one else wrote books like me, and I thought … well, I bet I could teach some people how, and humanity could benefit from better books being written.

Ultimately though, I wrote this book because it was fun, and I immensely enjoyed writing it.

I hope you love it and that it helps you on your creative journey. I hope all your dreams come true because you learn to write amazing fiction. Don't ever underestimate where it can take you.

Love,
Meg

For the dreamers who refuse to quit, even when it gets hard, and the readers who became writers because no one would pay them to read.

AUTHOR'S NOTE

This book isn't written in a linear fashion because creativity isn't linear. It's nonlinear, as is my creative process.

Who am I, and why might my creative process matter at all, and why should you take my word on how to write amazing fiction? My name is Meggan Wilson, but millions of people around the world know me best by my pen name, Meghan March, *New York Times* best-selling author. I started writing fiction in 2012. I know that doesn't sound like I've been at it for a long time, but since then, I've written more amazing fiction than most people will write in a lifetime. Of my 39 fiction titles currently published, we produced nine *New York Times* bestsellers, 11 *Wall Street Journal* bestsellers (including two #1s) and graced the *USA Today* bestseller list 36 times with 34 different titles. I don't keep track of the foreign bestseller lists, but my books have hit those, too, in some of the 15 languages they've been translated into so far.

I write books that people not only buy, but ones that they read and then beg for more. You could call me a literary crack dealer because that's how many of my readers feel about my work. They always want more. It's a blessing and something I've had to grow into, especially when it comes to learning how to handle the accompanying pressure.

When I started writing fiction in 2012, it was because I had been writing books since first grade and had wanted to write a romance novel since seventh grade. I decided to do it by the time I was 30. By 2014, when I published my first book, I'd altered my goal and enlarged it significantly. Not only did I want to write a romance novel, but I also wanted to make enough money writing novels so that I could quit my soul-killing job as a corporate lawyer. I had to replace a $150,000 annual income by writing and selling books. At the time, it seemed like a huge mountain to climb. How long would it take to build up a career that could support me so I could wake up every day and do something I loved, as opposed to something I hated?

It took me less than 15 months from self-publishing my first romance novel to the day I quit my job with two years of income saved in the bank—notwithstanding the fact that the first two books I had written and published were total flops.

How did I do it? How did I go from being a stressed-out corporate lawyer who hated her job to making millions of dollars from writing down the stories in my head—all in the space of a few years?

By writing amazing fiction.

By believing in myself, no matter what anyone else thought.

By doing everything I was capable of doing to give myself the best chance to live the life of my dreams.

Now, I live a life beyond my wildest dreams. Back then, I had no idea life could get this good. I honestly didn't even know it was possible.

I've sold over five million books in less than a decade—and stopped counting when I hit five million. I have readers and fans all over the world. People literally wish they could be me and live my life. It's quite a trip.

The only reason I mention all of this is to give you a sense of who I am and why I'm writing this particular book. I know I'm not the only person who has dreamed of quitting their day job and becoming a full-time author with a thriving career and income. As part of my way of giving back to those who are still dreaming the same dream I once had, I'm offering you what I know, which I believe could be of use to you on your journey—my most valuable insights, my methods, how I think, what I do, my secrets, and my tips, tricks, and troubleshooting fixes. I've packed as much information about my process and my mindset into this book as I could—all while going through the creative process myself as I begin work on my fortieth fiction title.

Every author's creative process is—and should be—different. We are all different. We all work with creative flow differently. My process is my process, and it's constantly evolving. I am a student of continuous improvement. I'm always trying to find ways to work more efficiently, effectively, and write better books.

All of what I offer within these pages might or might not work for you. But like I've done with all my research on writing, craft, mindset, and my many, many conversations with brilliant, successful, and talented authors, I hope you take what resonates with you and leave the rest. Creative processes can always be improved. Books can always get better. Authors should never stop learning.

I offer this book to you with love and hope. I wish you the best in your writing, your career, and your life. It's a wild adventure that never stops evolving. I hope yours is an amazing ride.

Cheers and happy writing,
Meg

INTRODUCTION

Writing a book isn't nearly as daunting as it seems. The most important thing to know is this: if you don't feel like you know what you're doing, join the club. I've written and published 39 fiction titles and two nonfiction titles, and I still don't feel like I "know what I'm doing" when it comes to writing books. Every single time I sit down to start a new book, I wonder, *Do I actually know how to do this? Can I actually finish this?*

I felt that way after finishing my first book while embarking on my second, and I still have those same questions occasionally floating in my mind as I begin my fortieth fictional work. I've felt that way about every single book in between as well.

Get used to the feeling, but don't let it stop you from doing it anyway.

Writing books really isn't that hard. In fact, the hardest part, in my experience, is getting yourself to sit down and actually work.

Nora Roberts, a legend in the fiction realm, put it this way: "Butt in chair. Hands on keyboard." That's literally the most important part.

The idea in your head—which is amazing, no doubt—will never be experienced by another soul unless you sit down, put your hands on the keys, and start working your magic.

And the creative process *is* magic.

You're not writing this book alone even if you're toiling away solo at your computer. You're never alone when you're creating. Ever. Creative flow is right there with you, every single step of the way. It's showing you where you need to go and giving you the words to fill the page—even if you think you're the only one working. You're not.

We were created to create. I believe that's why we're here, being human. We're learning and growing, and we're creating our own realities around us at every moment of the day. In many and varied ways, creativity is a natural ability that we're all blessed with.

I'm a storyteller. I've been a storyteller since I was a child. I would come home from school, retelling the stories of books and movies I'd been exposed to in great detail to my family, and then I would make up stories about my dolls, my stuffed animals, and even the deacon and priest during church service.

This is something I was born to do, but I'm certainly not the only one. There's a storyteller inside everyone, if you want to bring it out.

Since you're reading a book about writing amazing fiction, I'm assuming that you're already there and you want to learn how to take that magical idea in your head and turn it into something that can be read and enjoyed by others. And maybe even make a living at it so you can be a full-time creative artist. It's an amazing life to live, I must say, although it's not without its unique challenges and requirements.

So, how do you start? How do you go from aspiring author to actual author?

I believe it all starts in your heart and your mind. You have a dream, a desire, something that is calling you forward to greener pastures and a more fulfilling experience of life. That's coming from your heart. Those heart-centered desires are magical. They're the yearnings of your soul, begging you to become more of who you are in truth and let your soul shine its unique light in this world.

What stops us from just taking the leap and *doing it* then? That's where your mind comes in. It's an excellent tool and servant, but a terrible leader and master. Your mind is extremely powerful, but it has to be directed by your heart for the best outcomes. That's a lesson that took me many years to learn.

While you might know you desperately want to write amazing fiction, your mind can still get in your way. How?

Self-doubt.

It's a doozy. It's something that pretty much every creative artist has to contend with at some point—or every day.

Perhaps you even have a great idea already. It's been swimming around in your mind, gathering steam and details. Maybe you can even see the characters and the scenes playing out in your mind's eye, and it's *so real*. But then, when you sit down and face a blank page or screen, you might feel totally intimidated and completely overwhelmed.

It's not just you. It's all of us. We've all felt that. You're in good company. Welcome, sit down, and enjoy because there's a lot of awesome stuff to come.

The first part of writing a book is all mental. You have to believe you can do it. You have to believe it's possible for you. You have to believe in yourself. You have to believe the time and effort you put into this project will be worthwhile. You have to develop the discipline to see it through. That will require getting comfortable with self-doubt and not letting it derail you from creating something that has never existed before.

Because that's what you're doing—creating something unique and original that doesn't currently exist.

Even if it's an old idea that's been around forever—because there is truly nothing new under the sun when it comes to fiction—your creation will still be unique and original because *you've* never written it before.

You are the key ingredient. It's *you* who makes it unique because you are unique. No one else has ever had all your life experiences. No one else sees the world exactly the way you do. No one else can tell the story of your heart the way you can because *it's your story*.

We are all created equally, but none of us are the same. We are all totally unique, and we are all on unique paths through life that will yield unique results and unique creations.

If you're worrying that your idea isn't good enough, interesting enough, or whatever enough, *stop*.

It's in your heart and your mind for a reason. If you can accept that and understand *you* are the only person who can bring that idea to life and into concrete form other people can experience, then your story will become a whole lot more interesting.

No one else can see what's in your head. No one else can feel your characters the way you can. They are *yours* for a reason. The question is, are you brave enough to commit to the process of bringing them to life so that they can live in truth and be experienced by the masses?

Being a creative artist takes courage. Being willing to put your ideas on paper and offer them to the world as a gift takes *a lot* of courage. Give yourself a giant high five if you're going to take this step because you have to know that many people are not nearly as brave as you are.

Tons and tons of people have stories in their heads. *Tons.* As an author, I hear it all the time. People love to tell you about the story they would write if they *only had the time* or if they *only knew how*. Often, they'll ask you to write it—and share the royalties with them, of course.

My reply is always this: "It's your story; you should write it."

No one can give me a story to write. I don't work that way. I can't do it. My stories arise organically, springing from my interests, the depths of my soul, the insane workings of my mind, and the mysteries of my heart. I have to be totally, completely, ardently in love with the idea in order to be able to make space, find the energy, commit the time, and dredge up the discipline to bring that idea to life. It takes *a lot* for me to do that. The story has to be *epic.* It has to come from my heart and feed my soul. Otherwise, the process is just too painful to bear for any other reason.

Maybe I shouldn't say that, especially this early in the

book, because I don't want to scare you away. But I'm committed to being totally honest, open, and authentic about what writing amazing fiction truly is for me.

Amazing fiction isn't written to be on trend. It isn't written purely for money.

It has to be written for the love of the story. That's the first key. This story will be your companion for days, weeks, months, or *years*. You have to think it's amazing enough to spend that much time with it and to nurture it into becoming all that it can be. You have to be willing to make sacrifices for your story. You have to be willing to work and work *hard*. You have to be willing to do whatever is in the best interest of the story. I imagine it's not unlike giving birth to a child and raising it. There are tons of joy and happiness, but there's also pain and sacrifice often required to get to those magical words *The End*.

This is why not just any idea will do. It has to be an idea you're passionately on fire about because that's the type of energy it takes to write amazing fiction.

If you're not passionately in love with your story, readers might not be either. If you think your story is boring, readers might think it is too.

This story is part of you. The book you leave behind will be part of your legacy. Give it your best. Make it amazing. It might not be easy, but it'll be worth it.

PART ONE

PREPARATION

ONE
IDEATION AND CHOOSING YOUR BEST BOOK IDEA

I love ideation. This is the most fun part of writing books for me. I *love* living in my head, playing make-believe, watching random scenes play out, meeting characters, trying on possibilities, and letting plot ideas unfold. I love playing around with my imagination, which runs wild and seemingly has no bounds.

Your imagination, as you might have guessed, is a huge key to writing amazing fiction. And so is spending lots of time *thinking* about your idea.

I'm a deep thinker by nature. I used to be addicted to thinking. I didn't even know that was a thing, but it turns out that it is. However, when you make your living by creating worlds and characters in your head, deep thinking is very useful and can be very lucrative. While I spend much less time thinking these days than ever before in my life, when I do spend time thinking, it's intentional and with purpose.

Creativity doesn't happen without your full participation. Ideation doesn't happen without your participation either. You have to make space in your personal world for ideas to come to life. You have to be open and aware so that you don't miss them when they pop up. This is what the ideation process is all about. If your mind is full of worry about drama, gossip, TV, work, friends, family issues, business, stress, and other stuff, it can be much harder to find the necessary mental and emotional space to ideate—not to mention, the time it takes.

For best results, I suggest intentionally clearing out your mind and blocking out everything else in the world in favor of spending time thinking about your amazing book idea. In my experience, the more time one puts into ideation and preparation, the easier it is to write an amazing story.

Ideation doesn't have to be fancy. It can be—and often should be—very simple. I prefer brain-dumping everything about my idea into writing, whether on a computer, in notes on my phone, or—my favorite—with old-school pen on paper in a journal.

When you start writing down all your ideas, you're already tapping into the magic of creative flow. You're investing time and energy by writing them down. It's an intentional act that tells the Universe that you're serious about your creativity and your book idea. As a result of that intentional act, more ideas, details, and bits and pieces of the story will continue to flow your way. You don't even have to look at those notes again either, if you don't need to or want to. When I write things down, it helps concretize the idea in my memory, so much so that I don't usually have to look back at my notes, but your process might be different.

Either way, writing things down makes them real. Writing down everything you know about your idea is the easiest way to get started. Don't be surprised if more information starts flowing your way as soon as you start writing what you already know. The more energy and attention you feed your idea, the more steam it will gather until it becomes its own entity. It becomes magnetic, bringing more and more details to you to add to your notes. With more time and more mental space and energy devoted to thinking about your idea, eventually, you will have a story that's ready to write.

You can also totally decide to skip this mental-marinating part if you already have an idea and want to get right to it and figure the story out while you're writing it. You can get hit with a flash of inspiration, open a new document, and just start writing.

This is what I did with my first book. I learned some really important lessons by trying this method. Namely, it can be really hard to figure out what you're writing about, why you're writing it, where you're heading, how it's going to come together as a readable story, and how you're going to finish it.

After taking that track once, I decided I would never do it again because it was like setting off on a journey with no map and no compass. It took me two years to figure out how to write my first book, and I struggled a lot with the process. I had no idea what I was doing. I was just *doing it*. I spent a ton of time procrastinating because I didn't know where I was headed or even what the point of the story was. I was just meandering from scene to scene, wondering if I was writing a book.

If that sounds familiar, don't lose hope. I eventually finished that book, and it turned out pretty great. I learned a *ton* during the process, and I'm sharing everything I learned then—and through writing 38 other fiction titles—here.

These days, I don't sit down to start writing a story until I've thought about it for at least six months. Sometimes, it's a year—or many more—of thinking before I write a single publishable word for a story. If that sounds insane and you're thinking, *I don't have that kind of time or patience*, know that I used to be the person who constantly said, "Patience is not my virtue," at every opportunity. Patience, as it turns out, can not only be learned, but it's also a really, really useful virtue. Especially when it comes to creativity and writing amazing fiction.

It also helps to know that story ideas get more awesome with time. It takes time for ideas to percolate and unfold in your mind. I call this "letting the pot simmer." I imagine my mind to be like a stove, and at any given time, I have many pots on that stove. Some of them are brand-new ideas that have just come to me. I'm usually entranced by the shiny, new idea and adore thinking about it. When I've reached the end of everything I know about the shiny, new idea—and written it all down—I put the lid back on the pot and let it simmer and attract more pieces that will help it to become a full-blown story someday.

Other ideas have been simmering in pots for *years*. They're still not ready yet. Only time will tell when those ideas are fully cooked and ready to be born, but that's not part of the process I control or will ever try to control again. I've learned the hard way that, just like a rushed and hurried meal, a story you try to throw together and grind onto the pages with as little time and effort as possible will be a much less palatable creation for you as the creator. It can be downright painful to write a story that isn't ready yet. I've done it. It sucks. It's also my least favorite book I've ever written.

Perhaps I'm unusual in this respect because I know there are authors who can get hit with a flash of new inspiration, dive in, and let an entire book pour out of them in days—and that's *awesome*. If you're one of those people, then kudos. Live it up and run with it. Your process will be different than mine, and that's perfect for you.

It's just not how I write fiction.

My stories take time. They're layered. They're complex. They're intricate. They're also amazing, and people love them and read them over and over again, coming back to the characters like they're old friends they haven't seen in a long time.

I write for the rereaders because I'm a rereader. I want everything I create to be memorable, magical, and moving. I don't want to write fluff books that someone forgets the second they read *The End* and close it. That's not for me. I've read plenty of those forgettable books, and I couldn't tell you who wrote them, who the characters were, what they were about, or if they had any particular impact on me. I've also never recommended any of those books to my fellow readers.

But then there are my favorite stories. The books I read decades ago that I can still tell you all about the characters, the plot, and how it made me feel. *Those* are the kinds of books I endeavor to write. Books that stay with you. Books that matter to you. Books that you're grateful were written. Books that are *amazing*.

Books like that take a lot of thought, energy, and attention up front. They take effort to bring to life. They take work, and they take believing in magic.

They also all start with ideation.

So, how do you do it? It's literally as easy as thinking about it. I call it "stirring the pot in my head." When I have some free time and mental space, I lift the lid and dive inside.

Sometimes, I just think. I think about the setting and see it more clearly, letting more and more details filter in and populate the image forming in my mind's eye.

Sometimes, I freewrite all my thoughts out, in no particular order. I just get all the ideas and details written down so I don't lose them. The notes don't have to be coherent or make sense to anyone else, just to you, the creator.

Ideation all comes down to spending time with your idea and devoting the necessary mental energy and attention to thinking about it and ruminating on it. When you do that, you're telling the Universe that this idea and this story is important to you because you're putting your attention on it. Where attention goes, energy flows. Energy is what it takes to create and expand on amazing ideas. Your attention is *key*. You can't create an amazing story without spending *tons* of attention on it. You get out what you put in. Take the time to think about your ideas. I promise that even if they feel flat and two-dimensional when you start, if you spend time thinking about them, they're going to grow and expand and become something completely different by the time you're ready to start writing.

Give yourself time and space and let your imagination run wild. Write it all down. The pieces will probably not come to you in order. That's okay. It doesn't matter. Ideation for writing amazing fiction often feels like you're getting puzzle pieces handed to you one at a time. You might have no idea what the picture you're putting together will even look like. That's okay too. It doesn't matter. All that matters is collecting the pieces, thinking about them, playing with them in your mind, and giving them time to weave together into something brilliant that has never existed before.

This is not science. This is an art form. You are an artist. No one can tell you exactly how to ideate for your best outcome. It's something you're going to have to try and see how it goes. It's an adventure. You have no idea where it might lead you. Grab the pieces as they come, drop them into your pot, and keep stirring until that story is fully cooked and ready to be served.

It's a process. Trust it. Believe it is leading you somewhere awesome. And it will. If you haven't made it to awesome yet, just keep going. You'll get there. And you might even cultivate some patience along the way.

Where Do You Get Your Ideas?

This is the question I get asked most often as an author, and it's likely the most often asked question for any author. Everyone wants to know where you get your ideas.

I answer honestly, "Everywhere and nowhere."

I have no idea most of the time. It can be anything. A song's lyrics. An overheard conversation. A flash from the ether that bursts into my mind. A random thought that just hits right. Ideas are magical. They fly around constantly, and to catch an amazing one, you just have to be open to it.

Tell the Universe you want to write an amazing story and you need an incredible idea. And then be receptive, open, curious, and aware and see what happens. The Universe is always listening to you, and it is a vital partner in all your creative efforts. The Universe *is* creative flow. You're working with the unseen majesty that exists all around us, and you become an antenna for it when you tell it that you're open and willing to receive something awesome.

All you have to do is intend to come up with an amazing idea and then be actively waiting, ready to pounce on something that comes your way and gives you the feeling that it's *the one*.

That's pretty much how it works. It's not really altogether too complicated. I think people want it to seem more complicated because, somehow, if there were more steps or parts to the process, it might be easier for the mind to grasp. But the reality of it is much simpler. Ideas are everywhere, all the time. They're just waiting for your receptivity, notice, and attention.

Your initial idea will grow, evolve, change, and expand in a myriad of different ways. Sometimes, the initial idea I have for a story—the very spark that starts the whole process—doesn't even end up in the book.

Why? Because after that growth, evolution, change, and expansion, the initial spark wasn't in the best interest of the story. And if you want to write amazing fiction, the thing that will always matter most is, *What is in the best interest of the story?*

Notice I said, *What is in the best interest of the* story?

Not, *What is in the best interest of the* author?

They aren't always the same thing. There have been plenty of times when I have had to sacrifice something I wanted to keep—kill my darlings, as the saying goes—because it just didn't serve the best interest of the story anymore.

You have to be willing to flow and grow with the idea. It might take you places you never expected to go. That's okay! In fact, that's *fabulous*. An idea that becomes a story that's unpredictable for the author will also be unpredictable for the reader. That's *great*! Readers love being shocked and surprised. It's one of the keys to making fiction amazing, in my view.

There's a Robert Frost quote I read many years ago that stuck with me: "No tears in the writer, no tears in the reader. No surprise in the writer, no surprise in the reader."

Let your ideas surprise you. It's fun and exciting, and it keeps you even more engaged in the process. Don't try to control where the story goes. Let it play out on its own. You're a passenger on this ride even if it feels like you're supposed to be the pilot. You're really not. You're cocreating with creative flow, and creative flow is *full* of surprises.

Enjoy this part of the process. Give it time. Ask the Universe for help. Be patient. Be open to receiving those incredible ideas from the Universe. Pay attention to those flashes of inspiration that hit you just right. Write them down! Think about them. Give them your attention. Let your ideas marinate. Let them simmer. Play with them in your mind. Let them grow and expand and become more and more layered and rich and *real.* That's where all great fiction starts—with an inspired idea.

Yours is out there. You just have to be open to it.

Your Best Book Idea

Not all book ideas are created equally. You will likely have *many, many* book ideas in your life. That's fantastic! How do you decide which idea to write first?

That's something only you can decide. I follow my excitement and what sounds like the most fun to me. That's the compass I've used my entire literary career, which has led me to extraordinary success. I don't pick book ideas based on what sounds like it will make the most money or sell the most copies. I have before, and those books were ultimately more painful to write, and they did not deliver the results I had hoped to achieve. Writing the stories of my heart and soul— the stories that I don't care if anyone else loves because I love them so much that it doesn't matter—has changed my life irrevocably. It's given me financial freedom and allowed me to live every day in a reality that is beyond any fantasy I could have ever conjured up about my life.

Listen to your heart. Pay attention to how it feels when you're considering your potential book ideas. Which idea makes your heart feel like it's expanding, growing, or has suddenly sprouted wings? Which idea gets you the most excited? Which idea feels like it has the most breadth, depth, richness, and color? Which idea feels like it can sustain an entire book? Which idea can you not stop thinking about and playing with in your mind?

Those are all good clues to follow when selecting your best book idea for *right now*. Remember, you can write *all* your ideas. It's just a matter of time and effort. But you have to start with *one*. Pick the idea you *have to* write because you can't *not* write it right now.

What about that shiny, new idea you just got though? You're on fire with excitement about it, and it knocked your previously most favorite idea off the top of the podium.

Remember this: every new idea is a shiny, new toy and you're a kid who can't wait to play with it. So, play with it. Brain-dump everything you can possibly think of about the new idea into a journal or document or note until you run absolutely dry. Then, reread everything you wrote. Does it sound like there's enough to dive into a book *and finish the book*?

Every shiny, new idea can seduce you. After all, shiny, new ideas are one of the most fun parts of being a creative. We all love shiny, new ideas. It's a high you ride, and it's totally addictive.

The trick to turning those seductive, shiny, new ideas into amazing fiction is knowing which one to write and when, along with having the discipline to see that particular idea through until it's a fully-formed book.

If you constantly jump from idea to idea—starting book after book, but finishing none—you aren't writing amazing fiction. You actually have to finish a book to do that.

And, yes, we've all been in the same position. The book you're working on was once a shiny, new idea that you were seduced by and excited about. Remember that. It's an easy fact to forget once you're in the trenches, doing the actual work to bring the idea fully to life. While it might not be as seductive and exciting as the flash of inspiration and falling in love with the shiny, new idea, it's an integral part of the process you cannot skip.

Many, many creatives have lots of unfinished manuscripts. Authors who write amazing fiction have lots of *published books*. There's a massive difference there.

To be clear, however, I'm not saying you should resist the temptation of a new idea at all. But, you must be strategic and disciplined about bringing it to life.

This is why it is absolutely critical to pick your *best idea* and run with it. Your best idea is going to be the idea that can sustain you creatively for an entire book or even more than one book. That kind of idea has depth and staying power. An idea might start off as a tiny seed, but just like an apple tree, it is capable of becoming so much more than its humble beginnings and bearing much fruit. But just like an apple tree, you have to pick which seed you're going to plant and water it, take care of it, and give it your time, attention, and love. You can't suddenly decide you want to plant another seed and take care of that tree while letting your previous plant wither and die.

Pick an idea you can see through to *The End*.

My best advice on this subject is to listen to your heart and use it like a compass. It'll take you where you need to go. Sit with your ideas. Which one really feels like it makes your heart sing? Ignore your mind and all the rationalizations it will often throw at you for why you should write a different book instead of the one your heart wants. Your mind doesn't know how to make your dreams come true. Your heart does. It just communicates differently and is much quieter than your mind. But still, take the time to really *feel* which idea is the winner for you to write right now.

Also, make sure you save *every single seed* that comes to you. You have no idea how those seeds could combine and turn into something even more brilliant.

Many times, I have had a shiny, new book idea that seemed like it might be its own separate book, and somehow, it ended up being an unexpected piece of the puzzle I was already working on, not its own new book. Creativity is not linear. Often, you have no idea where or how the pieces will fit together. That's totally fine. It will become clearer as you continue going forward. Eventually. Be patient. Keep an open mind. Always be receptive to awesome ideas from the Universe even if you have no clue what you're going to do with the idea when you receive it. Those ideas are treasures. Cherish them and be happy you keep getting them. You don't know where they could lead you. That's just part of the creative adventure.

TWO
CHARACTERS

Characters are real. At least, *great characters* are real. What is a great character? In my opinion, as a diehard reader for over 30 years, it is a character that is relatable, memorable, multidimensional, well written, flawed, layered, and well developed. Great characters make amazing fiction. You can't have amazing fiction without great characters. It's just not possible.

How do you make sure your characters are great?

There are many different ways great characters can come into being, but most of my experience comes from two specific paths: (1) characters you create with the assistance of creative flow and (2) characters that storm into your mind, fully formed and ready to cause a ruckus.

Creating Characters

How do you create a character?

It's a process, just like writing a book. Preparation is key.

Patience is key. My best characters develop over periods of time—months or years—simply from thinking about them occasionally (or a lot).

If your ideation process produces a plot idea for a story but the characters have been left blank in your mind, then you will start creating them from the story idea.

Once upon a time, I was on a flight to New Orleans for a mergers and acquisitions seminar, paid for by my law firm, when I was hit with an idea about a girl who was running away from her life—something I wanted to do at the time. She was going to New Orleans, and she was going to live in the French Quarter and start a new life. The seed of that idea included only the very basics of the character—a girl running away from her life to live in the French Quarter.

I had no idea who she was or why she would do such a thing. But that's a question easily answered when you're a creative soul. All you have to do is pull out one of the most important tools in your toolbox: *ask yourself questions*. Start with the most important one: *why?*

Why was she running away from her life? Why was it so important she change her identity and hide from her past?

I didn't write any of this stuff down. I just ruminated on it during my flight. By the time the plane touched down in New Orleans, I knew she was one of the most hated people in America because of something her father had done and they thought she was also involved. From there, I skipped almost the entire seminar so I could walk the streets of the French Quarter and see what she would see and experience what she would experience.

I walked for days. With each step, I built a world in my

mind around this character who'd come to me as part of that idea on the plane. It was magical. Truly one of the most special creative experiences I'd ever had. I accepted the seed that had been planted into my mind on the flight, and I turned it into a seven-book series that grew organically—which ended up grossing over a million dollars and included my first bestseller.

I didn't know any of that could happen to me when I was sitting on that plane, in my economy seat, eating peanuts. All I did was take the idea that had popped into my head and started asking myself questions about who this girl was.

Why would she do what she did? What would motivate a person to do such a thing? What if *this* happened? What if *that* happened?

Asking yourself questions about the ideas that come into your mind is really important, especially *why, how,* and *what if.* But it's also important to know it isn't really you asking yourself the questions at all. It's actually you working with creative flow and cocreating something awesome, whether you realize it or not. When you take that idea—that seed—and focus your attention on it, you start unraveling an entire mystery for yourself and your readers. It's a beautiful process. One that should be enjoyed as much as possible for best results.

This part has nothing to do with making money or hitting lists. This is truly an organic creative process, where you and the Universe work together to create something that has never existed in form before. And the only way it is *going to exist* is if you devote your attention to it.

This question-and-answer process can happen on paper, if

that's what is easier and feels right for you. Don't ever discount the simple magic that can be created from the act of touching pen to paper. It truly is an act of alchemy because you're taking ideas that exist in the ether and you're bringing them through your body—through your lens of all your life experiences and your particular personality characteristics—and creating something new. It's an exciting process and truly magical.

Yes, it can also feel like work. But then again, so can counting stacks of money. It's all about the intention behind it and how excited you are about it.

If you're excited about getting to know this new character, then there's a way better chance your readers are going to be excited to get to know this new character too. You're just the first to make the discovery. And that discovery is like finding a new species or a new continent. This character has never existed in quite this way ever before because it's coming through *you*, and you are utterly and completely unique. There is no one else out there who is exactly like you. Which means there is no one else out there who can create exactly the same character you can create.

Spend time with your characters. It's the only way you're going to unravel the mystery, get to know them, and unlock the magic of the story they're carrying within them.

As you can tell, I don't "create" my characters by myself. I can't just sit down and say, "Okay, this book is going to be about a 35-year-old female who loves gardening and lives on a mountain, and her hero is going to be a 40-year-old man she meets at the grocery store."

I'm bored already, just writing that.

My decade of experience has shown me that if I'm bored during the process—at any point—then there's a good chance my readers are going to be bored too. If you're excited, there's a really good chance your readers are going to be excited. Tap into the excitement. It will flow into your creation. Plus, following that feeling has always led me to where I need to go creatively.

Can you create stories and characters by just picking names, ages, and occupations and then rolling forward with that? Sure. You absolutely can. Authors do it every single day. There are probably millions of books written just like that. But you're here to learn how to write *amazing* fiction. Not boring, two-dimensional, formula-based, commoditized fiction.

You have the option to create art. To create something people will remember and think about. Something that just might change someone's life. I'm here to tell you *that* is way more fulfilling as an author, and as it turns out, it can be quite lucrative too.

Readers—at least, *my kind* of readers—have been around the block. They've read tons of books. They're waiting for the next one to *wow* them. Those are the books readers get excited about. Those are the ones they can't put down. Those are the ones they *always* finish and then wait with bated breath for the next amazing book that they hope will give them that same thrill they got from the last book. That's how amazing fiction careers are born.

It all starts with inspired ideas and great characters.

Your reader needs to be able to identify with and relate to the character. If your characters are boring cookie-cutter cardboard contraptions, they won't be beloved by human readers who are unique and flawed and created as works of art by life itself. You have to give readers something to relate to. They don't want perfection. They want to lose themselves in a story where *they* are the character taking the adventure and learning the lessons. They want to forget themselves, allow reality to be suspended, and become someone else for just a little while.

Creating great characters is an homage to your readers. If you want to have lots of readers, you have to respect them and give them greatness. You can even give them a character who they might not even like, but are fascinated, intrigued, surprised, or enlightened by.

You only do that with attention, patience, and by being fascinated, intrigued, surprised, and enlightened by your characters yourself. You are your first reader. If you don't like the character and never connect with them, then there's a good chance your readers won't either.

When I was writing my breakout book, I knew I had work to do on the heroine to make her relatable and ultimately likable. After all, I had spent the first book in the series making her out to be an ice queen and a total rich bitch who was not likable at all. I didn't even like her in the first book.

But near the end of writing that first book, I'd realized she was going to be the heroine of the next story because she had major unfinished business with my next hero, with whom I was *totally in love.*

And, yes, this is how a series can grow organically. When you're writing, you have realizations that unlock new storylines, characters, plots, and subplots. Things that you, as the creator, didn't even know were coming, and quite often, they're very surprising. Which is great! Readers love surprises, and you should, too, as the author.

So, how did I take a thoroughly unlikable character and turn her into one of my most beloved heroines?

I made her relatable. I gave her demons, flaws, and issues that I knew my readers would relate to and for which they could find empathy. After all, *everyone* has a story. It's easy to write flat, one-dimensional assholes and villains, but they become great when you dig into their backstories.

How did they get like that? What forces in life shaped them to become the way they are? What are their fears? What are their dreams? What are their hopes? What makes them tick? How were they hurt? How did they internalize that pain? What caused the wound? How do they deal with it or overcome it?

Great characters have great backstories.

But here's the tricky part: the reader doesn't need to know —and won't ever know—as much about your characters as you do as the creator. One of the biggest rookie moves you can make while writing a book is to put every single detail of the character's backstory in writing, especially early on in the book. *Readers do not need to know everything you know to make the story amazing.* I maintain that readers probably should never know everything you know. It's just like a block of marble that contains a beautiful sculpture within it. The sculptor will reveal the beauty within, but he isn't going to bring all the chunks he carved off the marble to the museum to put them on display next to his art.

Patrons don't care about those excess scraps nearly as

much as they care about the beauty of the final sculpture before them.

Readers are the same way. They don't care nearly as much about every single detail you know in your mind as the author. They want to experience an incredibly written, colorful, deeply engrossing creation that allows them to suspend reality for a period of time. They don't need to know where your character went to second grade—unless that second-grade experience was absolutely vital to the character's development and necessary to explain why the character is the way he is to make some point in the story more real or more impactful to the reader.

You can save those little tidbits for behind-the-scenes stories about your creative process, or you can share things like that about the character *later—after* the readers have fallen in love with the character and are desperate to know any additional details you have held back and might care to share.

Writing amazing fiction is a balancing act. You don't know, even as the author, what details are going to be necessary for the story until you've got all those details about the character in your mind to paint the picture of who exactly this person is. Some details will make the cut, and others won't. Don't be afraid *not* to tell everything you know. It's an unappreciated art form.

Writing amazing fiction is totally nonlinear. You don't know what you're going to uncover about your characters or your story when you're thinking about it, giving it your attention, or writing it. It's truly like discovering the remains of Atlantis when you weren't even looking for them. You're just spending time and attention on thinking about the story and the characters, open to wherever the Universe leads you, and slowly, layer by layer, the characters will become very real, and the story will take on a life of its own.

This is how amazing fiction starts for me.

I'm a willing participant in the creative process. I'm the channel through which the story flows. I commit to giving the story my time, attention, patience, discipline, and effort. Then, creative flow comes in and helps me figure out the rest. I'm never creating anything alone. It's not possible. The very energy required to type these words and the very words themselves aren't coming *from* me. They're coming *through* me.

I don't decide what I'm going to write next, just like I don't decide who my character is going to be. It's a process of creating the necessary space in my mind and in my life to allow magic to happen. It also requires commitment and the dedication to see the story through. Full commitment is extremely important when working with creative flow. This is why the story idea must truly have your attention and get your excitement flowing.

The stronger your commitment, the more creative flow gets involved. If you receive a great character or idea and you do nothing with it and there's no commitment on your part to see it through, then don't be surprised if that character or idea goes elsewhere so the story can be born through someone else in some other way.

This has actually happened to me. My story idea and character ended up in someone else's book—someone I'd never met or spoken to—because I'd let the idea and character go when I decided not to write it.

Ideas are energy. They flow into us and around us, and if we do something with them, they flow *through* us into a form that has never existed before. But if we don't, that energy will move on. There's an excellent story about this in Elizabeth Gilbert's book on creativity, *Big Magic.*

Creativity is an active, dynamic process that is truly fascinating and incredible. The more I work with creative flow myself, the more utterly in love I am with being human and getting to experience it.

Writing amazing fiction will change you as an artist and a creator. It should. You should never be the same person you were before writing a book as you are after. If you are, then something was missing from the process. And that something, I believe, is your soul.

Amazing stories come from your soul. And by giving voice to the characters in that story, you're allowing your soul to live more fully and freely in the world, whether you realize it at the time or not.

This is why I say that great characters are *real.* They have flaws, needs, hopes, desires, and fears, just like nonfictional humans do. They're messy. They make mistakes. They screw up. They learn lessons. They grow. They evolve. They change. They aspire. They inspire.

You might think you're just writing a book, but you're participating in the very evolution of life by exercising your own creativity. Wild, right?

Receiving a Fully Formed Character

First, it is 100% possible for a fully formed and well-developed character to simply walk into—or more likely *storm into*—your mind. It has happened to me multiple times, and when it does, hold on to your bootstraps because things are about to get *real*. These are some of my favorite types of characters to work with, but they're also the bossiest and most insistent, and they can take you to some really unexpected places that you might never have intended to go.

Receiving a character like this—because that's what it really is: *receiving*—is a wild ride and a lot of fun.

In the interest of full disclosure, I must explain the circumstances under which two of my fully formed characters came into my mind: I was under the influence of drugs. There's a reason that artists and creative types talk about the effects of their drug use on their art, and that's because drugs can have a massive impact.

I am not, in any way, encouraging drug use. I would never do drugs just to put myself into a certain state to receive a character like this. However, it just so happens that I have enjoyed certain recreational drugs, and they have had a direct and definite impact on my creative work. I can't pretend they haven't just to make this book more politically correct.

Another one of my fully formed characters stormed into my mind when I was drunk. Again, I would never encourage the use of alcohol for this purpose. I don't drink at all anymore. But I can't discount the fact that getting blasted on Coco Loco in the Dominican Republic played a huge role in receiving one of my most memorable and reader-beloved characters of all time.

Since we're on the topic, I'll share my own personal theory as to why drug and alcohol use can spawn fully formed characters. Drugs and alcohol affect your consciousness and put you into an altered state. They all affect your vibration and consciousness in different ways, with some raising it and some lowering it. Your vibration and your consciousness are responsible for the events, people, and circumstances you attract into your life. I believe your vibration and consciousness are also what attract book ideas and characters into your life as well because they are simply energy too. When you alter your consciousness, whether through meditation, prayer, or recreational drug and alcohol use, you are tapping into different wavelengths in the zero-point field and bringing different experiences into your life.

If you want more discussion on energy and how all that works, check out *A Creative Rebel's Guide to Winning the Game of Life*.

Suffice it to say, however, how you feel, what you do, and your state of being will all influence your creative work and the rest of your life. When you're high or drunk or even praying or meditating, you are in an altered state. When you're in that altered state, you have access to things that you don't have access to in your normal state. That's how my fully formed characters were able to storm into my mind—I was in an altered state.

Because I was in an altered state, induced by vibration-lowering substances, it's no surprise that all three of the heroes I received this way were strong, dominant alpha males who had serious issues of their own that would need to be brought to light, worked upon, and shifted throughout their stories so they could evolve into healed men.

Ultimately, this is what you're doing with your characters —recognizing their flaws, bringing them to awareness, and allowing the story to unravel, unpack, and heal those wounds so they can reveal the beautiful treasures within them. It's not unlike what each of us is doing here on Earth—recognizing our flaws and wounds, bringing them to awareness, and using life to heal ourselves so we can discover the treasures within us.

Writing books is extremely therapeutic because of this, in my view. I've worked out many, many of my own issues within the bounds of a story by gifting those issues, insecurities, wounds, dreams, hopes, and fears to my characters. It's not something I did consciously at first, but eventually, I realized what I was doing and was grateful to have the means to sort through my own baggage within the pages of my books, whether anyone else ever realized it or not. Often, I was able to learn my lessons through my characters, as opposed to learning all those hard lessons through my own relationships and life.

Whether that's normal or not, I have no idea. But I suspect most authors do it, perhaps subconsciously though.

Bottom line: You *are* your characters. They are parts of you, however they are created or received. We are each the microcosm of the macrocosm. Everything that exists in this world—dark and light—exists within each of us. That's how you can create villains and assholes that you would never self-identify with. But that energy is within you, whether you're conscious of it or not.

If your characters aren't storming into your mind, which perhaps might be the less common way to meet your characters, but are still real and valuable, then you will create them. But at the end of the day, it really doesn't matter how your characters come into being. It just matters that they're *great characters*. That's what readers remember most. That's why readers go back and reread their favorite books over and over again, even when they know exactly what's going to happen. They adore the characters. That's why great characters are a necessary component to writing amazing fiction.

Interesting Side Characters

Interesting side characters are just as important as memorable main characters. Side characters can make or break a book. These are the friends, enemies, allies, and more. Side characters give you so much room to create unique voices and add humor and emotion to the story. They can act as a mirror or foil to your main characters. Also, great side characters often grow organically through the story and end up becoming reader favorites, who then might merit their own book. You never know what you're really creating. You might think it's a stand-alone book about two characters, but the side characters might end up being so powerful and awesome that they deserve a spin-off story of their very own. These are great stories to write because readers are already invested in the characters from the original book and often can't wait to find out more about them in their own book.

Here's a great nonbook example. With very, very, very few exceptions, I haven't watched a television show since 2014. One of those exceptions is *Letterkenny*. I've seen almost every episode. It's a hilarious and often vulgar Canadian sitcom, written in such a smart, engaging, and entertaining manner with incredible characters. Through many seasons, we were treated to an asshole side character named Shoresy. We really knew nothing about him, but as a storyteller, I had a feeling that Jared Keeso, the creator of the show and main actor, knew a lot more. Of course, I was thrilled when I heard they had released a spin-off show called *Shoresy*. I didn't even like Shoresy as a character in *Letterkenny*, but I loved the creations of Jared Keeso, so I was all in. When we watched the first season, I fell in love with Shoresy. His backstory and his character sealed the deal. As of this writing, I don't know if there will be a second season, but I really, really hope so because I loved Shoresy and his supporting cast of characters even more than I ever loved Letterkenny.

My breakout novel happened because of a side character. He was an epic character in my second release—which completely flopped—but I was totally in love with him. I had to write his story even if no one ever read it. It had to be told. So, I told it even though no one had asked for it or seemed to want it. I followed my gut and my excitement, and as always, it led me exactly to where I needed to go. That memorable, awesome side character in my flop became the hero that starred in my breakout novel.

Never underestimate the power of fabulous side

characters. Amazing fiction always has them. This is how an author can easily grow a series organically. Invest time, energy, and creativity into your side characters. Make them interesting. You never know where they might end up taking you—and your life.

Steal Like an Artist

When you're creating characters, steal like an artist. Borrow traits, characteristics, quirks, interests, issues, problems, habits, sayings, and more from people in your life, in your past, or in the media. I never borrow an entire person, but I take bits and pieces from *lots* of people.

That heroine I made everyone fall in love with? I borrowed her issues and a bit of her backstory from some girls I knew in high school. I didn't ask for permission. I have no idea if they'll ever read the book. Probably not. But if they do … it's highly unlikely they'll recognize the bits I borrowed from here and there, but who knows? However, I did have other people reach out to me and say that they had some of the *very same issues* in their pasts and connected with the heroine so strongly because of it.

By using real people's problems, issues, quirks, habits, interests, and more, you increase your chances of making the character feel real and relatable to your readers. Readers love characters they can relate to. They don't need to be able to relate to *everything*, but at least *something*. It makes readers more empathetic, and they want to root for the character to overcome all odds to triumph in the end. When a reader roots for a character, they want to know how the story ends. When a reader wants to know how the story ends, they finish reading the book. If they finish reading the book, there's a better chance they're going to read *another* one of your books. That's how amazing fiction careers work.

Be creative. Don't be too obvious. And above all, be kind. Don't steal something from someone's real life and then be a dick about it in your book, no matter how much you do or don't like them in real life. Mean-spiritedness doesn't engage readers the same way empathy does.

Your goal is to get readers to *relate* to the character, not feel shitty because you're making fun of or being judgmental about something they deal with or someone they love deals with in real life.

If you're struggling with your characters, develop an avid interest in life and pay attention to other people. Great characters are out there, and they come to life because you want them to come to life. Spend your time, energy, and intention on helping it happen. Allow them to form one layer at a time until they feel like a real person you might actually meet.

You can do it. I believe in you and the power of your creativity.

Naming Characters

I collect names constantly. I keep a running list at all times of unique and interesting character names. In fact, I've been adding to my list of fictional character names for over a decade. It's totally worth it, and tons of authors do this. Never underestimate the power of a great character name.

When I wanted to start writing a fantasy series, I found that my almost-decade-old list of names was insufficient though because I hadn't been in the market for fantasy-type names, so I hadn't added any that fit the bill to my list. A few years ago, I had to start completely fresh, specifically looking for great fantasy-type names that would resonate with my storyline.

I get character names from *everywhere*. One of my favorite places is from other people's books. Just don't make your *borrowing* of someone else's character names super obvious. We've already discussed stealing like an artist, and in the book, *Steal Like an Artist,* Austin Kleon talks about lifting pieces from here and there. That's exactly what I've always done. I'll take a first name from this book and a last name from somewhere else. Or in the case of some of my most beloved characters, I lifted names from colleges, street signs, and random people I'd met wearing name tags.

Everything is fair game when you're an author. As inspiration, you can use celebrities, athletes, neighbors, or the girl you didn't like in high school because you had a crush on her boyfriend—I've totally done that, and *no one* liked that character when the book was over. You can immortalize your grandmother or your dog—I've done both. What matters most about coming up with names for characters is that the name *fits* the character.

Often, I let the Universe name the main characters of the story. I find that just looking at my list of names and trying to pick a name for a hero or heroine feels too forced for me.

I have spent more than four years plotting a fantasy story without knowing either the hero's or the heroine's name. *Four years without names.* In my head, they were simply *initials.* That's all I needed to know in order to allow the story to percolate. However, when I was preparing to write the first chapter, I wondered, *Am I going to have to just pick names myself for them?*

Nope.

The Universe came through. The night before I wrote the first chapter, the heroine's name came to me. I didn't have to pick it out of a list. It was just ... there. Obvious. A name I'd loved for a long time that turned out to be perfect for her.

When I finished the first chapter, I wondered, *So, what's his name?* I'd been toying with a possibility for the hero's name for a year or so, but it just didn't seem to fit right. A few weeks after I wrote the first chapter, his name came to me too. Again, it was obvious and perfect. It just *fit.*

That's the most important part. *It has to fit.*

How do you know if it fits?

In my experience, a character name fits when the character couldn't possibly have any other name. It just *is them.* They embody the name. Also, it helps when it doesn't sound like it came from a soap opera, but I've done that too. Heck, even real people have soap-opera names sometimes.

One mistake rookies make pretty often when it comes to naming characters is this: they blow all the good names that they have saved up on every character in their first story. I did it too. I had all these side characters with *awesome* names.

I didn't realize that I'd only get to use that awesome name one or two times, and then we'd never hear from that side character again. It felt like a waste. Don't blow all your good names on characters who won't be heard from very often. Use them sparingly and sprinkle in some "normal" names so you have more fun ones to use later.

Be creative, but also don't go overboard with crazy names or similar-sounding ones. Take it easy on the reader. They have a lot to keep up with during your story, and you want to make sure they're following the story rather than tripping over or getting hung up on character names.

You want the character name to add to and enhance the story, not pull your reader out of the story, thinking about the weird or impossible-to-pronounce name you might have picked. If you've done that already, don't worry. I have too. It happens to the best of us.

Bottom line: You're the master storyteller here. You get to name everyone in this world or allow for them to be named by creative flow or the Universe. Have fun with it. Go with what feels right to you. If you can't think of the character by any other name than the one that's been in your head the whole time you've been plotting the story, then go with that. Changing it might mess with your flow.

However, if you're in a situation where you are writing a book with a unique and distinctive character name and you get word that another author is releasing a book around the same time with the exact same unique and distinctive name of your character, then you have a choice to make. Do you keep the name and not care that someone else will have the same hero or heroine name? Or do you rise above and find something even better to fit your character? I've had to change a hero's name with most of the story written due to a situation of this nature, and I'm actually really happy I changed the hero's name. I chose an even more unique and distinctive name that fit him even better. I would never have figured that out though had I not been challenged with the situation of potentially looking like a copycat if I didn't change it.

Use your judgment when naming. Keep a list. Keep it fresh. Add to it constantly. You never know where you're going to find inspiration, so keep an open mind all the time. If you're receptive to amazing character names, don't be surprised if they start to come into your world, courtesy of the Universe, without you having to do anything particular to dig them up.

Finally, I know a lot of authors who use baby-naming books to name their characters. *Lots of authors do this,* but I rarely do. Why? Because it feels forced to me. Plus, I don't like naming fully grown characters with names that have only become recently popular. How many 40-year-old Jaydens do you know? Probably not a lot, considering the name didn't become popular until long after they were born. Using today's trendy baby names on fully grown adult characters doesn't always make the most sense. If you're writing contemporary fiction, then look back at the names that were popular in the years around when your character was likely born. The internet has a treasure trove of information, including census lists of the 100 most popular names from each decade. It's a great way to keep older character names more believable, which is awesome if your story will require many a mind-stretching moment from your audience already.

But, as you'll read in an upcoming chapter, you're allowed to break all the rules. You're the master storyteller in your world. Ultimately, do whatever works best for you.

Flawed Characters

Your characters must have flaws. *Must.* No one is perfect—except for avatars like Jesus and Buddha—so your characters shouldn't be either. They need to have flaws. Flaws make them relatable and more likable. Also, you have to give your characters something to overcome so they can transform and grow throughout the story. Flaws are a great way to easily set up memorable transformative journeys for your characters. This goes for both heroes and heroines. Readers don't want to read about someone perfect. They don't know perfect people in real life, so perfect characters in stories aren't relatable.

Give them flaws! Give them quirks. Give them weird preferences and personalities. Make them interesting. Make them *real*. I constantly "borrow" behavioral characteristics from people in real life and give those characteristics to my characters. I borrow flaws. I borrow backstory. I borrow *all sorts of stuff* from real life. The most important part about this is blending the real with the fictional. Also, try not to use glaringly obvious characteristics from people if they're going to read the book. Or if you're going to, let the person know in advance.

I will often be talking to someone, and they'll be telling me a story, and I will straight-up ask if I can use what they said in a book. To date, no one has ever told me no.

Life is your muse. Inspiration is *everywhere*. Use it. Make your characters feel more real with flaws. Your books will be all the better for it.

THREE
GOALS, MOTIVATION, AND CONFLICT

Books have the power to change your life. I know this to be an absolute fact because my life has been changed by many books. One of the most important books that changed my life is called *GMC: Goal, Motivation, and Conflict* by Debra Dixon. I am insanely grateful to Debra Dixon for writing that book. Without it, I wouldn't be the author and creative artist I've become.

I was over a year and a half into writing my first book and spinning my wheels constantly because it just wasn't working. I was writing scene after scene—and rewriting scene after scene—but it didn't feel like it was going anywhere, and I had no idea how to end the book or make it something that people would actually want to read. Heck, I didn't even know how to make it something *I* actually wanted to read. I was just ... doing it.

Enter *GMC: Goal, Motivation, and Conflict* by Debra Dixon.

Talk about a wake-up call.

If you haven't read it or ordered a copy already, I highly suggest you do so. It might change your life too.

What about this book was so life-changing for me?

I learned the building blocks of great fiction. And those building blocks are, as you might have guessed, goals, motivation, and conflict.

Without those three things, you won't have amazing fiction. With those three things, you've got a fighting chance.

Debra Dixon's method is one I still employ today for every single new main character I write. Bar none. I do this *every single time* for each of my main characters before I start writing a new story. *Every single time.* It helps me *immeasurably.* I will not start a new story without figuring out the internal and external goals, motivation, and conflict for each main character.

So, how do you do it? First, do yourself a favor and read the book. It contains a treasure trove of incredible information that is vital to writing amazing fiction. I tell every aspiring author to read this book. For me, it was a *must* in getting to where I am. But before you do that, I'll explain how I personally use this method so you have an idea what I'm talking about.

First, I take out a giant easel pad and at the very top, I write one of my main character's names.

Across the top, beneath the name, I write INTERNAL and EXTERNAL. Down the left-hand side, I write GOALS, MOTIVATION, CONFLICT. Then, I draw lines to create boxes, and I know I've got magic waiting to happen in those six rectangles.

Do not underestimate the creative power you can unleash with this process.

I've had vague ideas or even well-detailed ideas that changed *completely* as soon as I started my GMC chart.

As you can tell, to create great fiction and have great characters, you have to know the internal and external goals, motivations, and conflicts for each main character. These are truly the building blocks of amazing fiction.

Goals

A main character must have a goal. There must be *something* they want out of life. You need to be able to articulate what that is.

For amazing fiction, a character must have external goals and internal goals.

An external goal is what gets the character moving, generally. It might be that the character needs money for something. Or possibly that the character needs something to happen. Or the character needs to find something. Or the character needs to prevent something from happening. It all depends on the story. The character can have more than one external goal. That's totally fine. But the external goal is what the character is seeking to accomplish out in the world. Whatever that external goal is, it needs to be *very important* to the character, and it needs to be urgent enough that they are going to take action to achieve it. This is how the story begins and what keeps it moving—the character has a goal, and they want it very badly, so they're willing to do things to achieve that goal.

The character's internal goal is what they are seeking for themselves that is intangible. Perhaps they want to satisfy an internal need that is emotional in nature.

Goals drive the story momentum. Amazing fiction includes a character wanting *something*. If the character is 100% content with their life and doesn't need anything to change in order to be wildly happy, then your story is probably going to be boring—although the character's life might be fantastic. Amazing fiction isn't generally about characters living perfect lives, where they have everything they want and need already. But if you can pull that off, kudos and more power to you.

I highly suggest reading Debra Dixon's explanation of this, as she is the master on this pivotal subject. Suffice it to say, character goals are wildly important. Characters must have goals. Character goals can conflict, which makes the story even more interesting. Regardless of whether they are conflicting, however, goals move the story along. They give the characters purpose. They create your plot and play into your pacing. They make writing amazing fiction possible.

Spend time thinking about and filling in your GMC chart. It helps create a clear picture of the story you're actually trying to write and helps you determine if it can truly sustain an entire book. My GMC charts are always a *key* part of my process. I refer back to them as needed, but I *do not* feel absolutely wedded to every single detail in the GMC charts while drafting the story.

The goals you write on this chart might end up changing as you write your story. It's okay. This is a nonlinear process. Be fluid. Go with what's best for the story while keeping in mind that the reader does want to be satisfied at the end by the character achieving *some goal*, but it's okay if it is not the *exact goal* the character set out to achieve in the beginning. You can still give the reader total satisfaction, especially if the original goal becomes impossible to achieve during the book.

Making your book match the GMC chart is not the point of the exercise. The point of the exercise is to get yourself really thinking about the story and how it's going to develop and unfold. Step one is knowing what your characters want. If you don't know what they want, internally and externally, then you don't really know them well enough to start writing about them yet.

I use GMC charts to get me to the point of clarity about the story, where I can finally begin the drafting process and get the words flowing. That's why I consider GMC charts to be absolutely vital to my creative process. They help me figure out enough things so I can get started on writing the book. The rest unfolds for me during the writing process.

Motivation

I say this all the time: "I can get a reader to believe *anything* as long as it is well motivated enough." And I mean it. It's the gospel truth.

You can get anyone to believe anything in fiction, but that requires *excellent motivation*—and timing and delivery.

But motivation is the most important.

Why does the character want what they want? What is their internal motive for wanting what they want? This might not be something the character ever tells anyone, but readers learn it through internal dialogue or the actions of the character. Why does the character want the external goal? This is hugely important. And remember, the bigger or more outrageous the goal, the more well motivated it must be.

If you're having trouble grasping this, think about yourself. Why do you want what you want? What gives you the motivation to go after it? What *moves* you? That's what motivation is. The thing that gets you to move.

Without strong motivation, characters aren't really moved to do anything, especially exciting, interesting things that make up amazing fiction. Motivation matters. Make sure it makes total sense to you—and hopefully someone else—but most of all, make sure the motivation will make sense to the reader. A weak or unclear motivation muddies fictional waters and makes it harder to suspend reality and believe in the events of the story. Make it clear. Make it *important.* The more motivated a character is, the more exciting the story becomes.

Also, not all motivations are created equal. Be creative here. This is where you can truly shine. However, never forget that some of the best motivations are simple—doing something to save someone the character loves or preventing something bad or painful from happening. Make sure whatever your character's goal is, that goal is extremely well motivated. The more well motivated the character is, the better your story will be.

If you want to put a character into a really terrible position and cause them to do something that might be *out of character*—which is often what great fiction does—you have to block off all their exits and options and leave them with only one visible path to take forward. But in order to get them to move down that path, they have to be motivated.

If the character doesn't take this step, is someone going to die? Will the character lose something that matters to them? Will the character miss out on some major opportunity? Will the character's honor be impugned?

The motivation behind everything a character does matters. It's not enough to write a character who acts like the majority of humans on this planet—unconsciously acting purely from habit with no thought at all behind their actions. That won't cut it for amazing fiction.

The character has to want something and want it *badly.* And the reason they want it badly has to be *extremely motivating.* If the character wants nothing badly, then the story probably won't move along at a good pace, keep a reader's interest, or be exciting enough for a reader to finish the book.

This is also a good point to mention that even a small goal can seem like life or death in fiction, if it's well motivated enough.

The motivation behind what a character wants is going to set the stakes of the story. High-stakes stories result in great fiction. What is going to happen to the character if they don't reach the goal? Whatever pain or tragedy or unhappiness that could happen is going to drive the motivation even higher. After all, just like a normal human, characters want to avoid pain, tragedy, and unhappiness. Those all make excellent motivations and can be played out in infinite, different scenarios and stories.

Why does the character want what they want? What will

happen if they don't get it? The more painful it will be for the character if the goal is not achieved, the greater the motivation to achieve it. That right there is a building block of amazing fiction.

Conflict

Conflict is the lifeblood of fiction. Without conflict, well-motivated goals would be easily attainable, and the story would either be short, boring, or both.

Conflict is everything that is standing in the way of the character achieving their goals. For great fiction, you need great conflict. It can't be stupid or contrived. It has to look, sound, and feel *real* to your character. This is where the stakes get higher and higher. The more daunting the conflict, the more the reader will be on the edge of their seat.

You have to put characters through hell in order to write amazing fiction. It doesn't have to be physical hell, but it has to be hell all the same. People learn in two ways—joy and pain. While I'm sure we'd all love to learn solely through joy, pain is an excellent teacher, and the lessons it teaches are not soon forgotten.

In order to write amazing fiction, you have to be able to create amazing conflict and put your character through pain. It sounds mean, and sometimes, it really sucks to do it, but just think about how different of a person you would be if you hadn't had some tough lessons in your life. Personally, the most tragic and terrible things that have happened in my life taught me some of the most memorable lessons and completely changed me as a human. Pain and suffering crack us open and break our hearts, but not out of cruelty. They break us open so we can allow more love into our lives and learn the lessons we came here to learn.

Your characters are here to learn lessons too.

In my view, the Divine Storyteller orchestrates the conflicts in our life—and we help that along through our thoughts, words, and actions—not to hurt us, but to teach us. To help us grow. To help us evolve. To help us reach our potential. It's unconditional love because the Divine Storyteller is not afraid to put you through pain if it ultimately serves a higher purpose in your life.

I know that might sound like someone who gets off on torture, but it's truly not like that.

You're not here to torture your characters into learning their lessons, and neither is the Divine Storyteller torturing you.

You're here to apply tough love to your characters so they can become the people they are meant to become through living this story. They're going to become stronger, wiser, kinder, more loving, more forgiving, and more surrendered to the magic that is life. Just like you are constantly being worked on by life to become all those things yourself.

You're just taking a page from the Divine Storyteller's book here and acting as a channel for creative flow to teach lessons to characters on your pages, possibly in hopes that a reader will learn those lessons without going through the same tragedies, pain, and suffering that the characters had to go through.

And, yes, I realize that's a rather high-level, spiritually oriented view of what you're doing that you might never think about ever again, but I believe it's true. You're a tool in the hand of the Divine Storyteller, and it is thrilled to be writing amazing stories through you. Your work serves a purpose. You're not just torturing your characters because you're a dick. You're putting them through hell so they will become all that they are destined to be.

Your story will only be as good as your characters and their goals, motivations, and conflicts. Make them meaningful. Make them memorable. But definitely don't worry that you have no idea what would fit those descriptions for your particular story right now. This is where we go back to remembering that we're not doing *any of this alone*. Even though I'm sitting here by myself, typing these words, creative flow is with me, prompting me on the next sentence and giving me guidance and direction. Every story you write is a cocreative effort. That's why I have no ego about my work. It's not just mine. I didn't create it solely by myself. My name might be on the cover, but without creative flow, there'd be nothing inside.

To create great conflict, make your GMC chart and spend some time with it. Give it your attention. Be open to whatever awesome ideas come to your mind and write them down. As soon as your pen hits the paper, you're actively working with creative flow.

Writing things down, especially on paper, unlocks a secret door to creativity that you cannot otherwise unlock.

If you don't know where to start with your goals, motivation, or conflict, start with pen and paper. Start by writing down the first question you need an answer to on the page.

For instance: *What is my hero's goal?*

Then, beneath it, start brain-dumping everything you can think of. Don't be surprised when your list starts to grow, and all of a sudden, something that feels inspired begins to make its way from your pen to the paper. I can't tell you how many times I've used this method and ended up with absolute gold. Hundreds of times. Perhaps thousands.

Just *write*. Let the ideas flow as a stream of consciousness. Make a list of them. Pay attention to which one gets you the most excited. That's a key indicator that I follow religiously. Excitement leads to magic. Also, don't be surprised if the ideas that excite or inspire you are totally not what you thought you were writing about in your book. That's *okay*. That's *amazing*. Don't stay wedded to your initial ideas if something better comes along. Granted, there will be things that are nonnegotiable that you feel you *must* include in the story, and that's great. But learn to be flexible. Learn to *flow*. I promise you that creative flow knows what it's doing. You just have to have the courage and fortitude to follow where it leads when it starts guiding you.

Writing amazing fiction includes a whole lot of magic. But much of that magic will just *appear* if you give yourself over to the process and invest your time and energy into it. Because that's what it is. A process. It will not be linear because life is not linear even though that's what our minds comprehend. When your story idea really starts gathering steam, you'll get pieces and parts that will fit in all different sections of the story. Chapter one doesn't always come first in the creative process.

Never underestimate the power of simple tools—paper,

pencil, pen, silence, solitude, commitment, patience, discipline, curiosity, open-mindedness, unbounded imagination, and playfulness. They are truly some of the most important parts of the process for me.

Get to know your characters. Spend time thinking about them. Ruminate on them. Daydream about them. Let them unfold. Learn to understand them. Fall in love with them. Become them.

That's a key to writing amazing fiction.

FOUR
REASEARCH

I'm committed to being totally honest in this book, and as a result of that commitment, I have to tell you, I don't do a lot of research. I do only as much research as is necessary to write the book. I think research is great and extremely necessary for certain genres and subgenres. However, I also think research is an easy place where you can get bogged down for ages and never make any progress on your book. Basically, research can be an awesome way to procrastinate.

If your story requires a ton of research to make it accurate and enthralling, by all means, *do it*. The last thing you want to do is publish something and get a bunch of crappy reviews because everyone wants to tell you every detail you missed or got wrong about the subject. This is especially true if there are many technical, historical, or procedural aspects of your story.

I find this can happen very often with anything that involves world history, police, the law, courts, sports, technology, et cetera.

Do as much research as you need to do in order to write the book. If you're in love with the research and it gives you joy, then take as much time as you want. Joy is a wonderful emotion to follow. But keep in mind that the goal is to write an *amazing story*. Be aware that if you do a ton of technical research and then try to insert every single technical detail into your book, you might bore your readers with stuff they don't really care about at all.

I once read a book about racing drift cars. I *love* cars. Absolutely. Totally. Completely. I was raised by a race car driver, so the love of fast cars and racing is in my blood. This book about drift racing had a ton of details about all the mechanical components and processes. It was really quite impressive how much research the author had done and how much firsthand experience the author clearly had on the subject. I loved that part, but even I, as a super car nut, got bored with some of the mechanical details. I read fiction for the love of the story, and I totally loved that I got my car-nut fix, but there is a fine line when it comes to including the right amount of details from your research in your story. It can be hard to resist the temptation to show off all your knowledge for the world, especially when you spent a lot of time and energy learning that knowledge. But remember, what's important here is *what is in the best interest of the story.* Not what feeds your ego, makes you feel special, or shows people you're an expert. Use your research materials in the book with care.

Contrast the book about drift car racing with one of my favorite car-related romances that involved Formula 1 racing, which gave me just enough of the color and flavor and technical aspects to satisfy my inner car lover without overloading me with more stuff than my gearhead self cared to know.

Keep your audience in mind when you're deploying your research throughout your book. Remember that while *you* might find every single detail that you're providing riveting, your audience is *not you*. Think about why they're reading the book to begin with. Are they reading for the escape? Then, maybe don't hit them with a character's gastrointestinal distress in the first chapter even though it's extremely realistic to the scene.

Readers get *plenty* of reality in their daily lives. They don't always want every single real detail in their fiction. Enough to make it real and believable, yes. But not so much that they have to slog through the details to get to the incredible story they're craving.

To sum up my stance on research, I'll say this: Do enough. Write the book. Ask your beta readers if they felt like you needed more details in any area of the book or about technical stuff that you included.

Oftentimes, they will say no.

Readers are there for the *story*. Not the research. Keep it relevant and keep the story moving. If they're reading fiction, most readers aren't there for a lecture. They want to be transported to another reality and to be entertained. That's your job. Keep that top of mind. It really helps when you're writing amazing fiction.

Setting: Using Real Places

Using real places can be amazing for a setting, but you have to do it well. This is where I do most of my research. If you can go to the place in person, do it. By walking around, getting the feel of a place and soaking up the energy of it, along with all the details—like the scent of the air and the cracks in the sidewalks—you're going to be able to make that setting come alive for your readers.

I can't tell you how many readers I've helped fall in love with the city of New Orleans. I fell in love with the French Quarter on a trip in 2014. By blowing off that mergers and acquisitions conference, I was able to wander the entire French Quarter, eating, shopping, and smiling my way through NOLA. It changed my life. That initial trip was ultimately responsible for not only the first seven book series it spawned, but also two trilogies and a duet. Plus, it resulted in many trips back to soak up more of the energy that is uniquely New Orleans. Readers constantly ask me if I lived there and are shocked when I say no. Even Louisiana natives are surprised that I've only visited a handful of times.

This kind of research obviously paid off for me, and I highly recommend if you are writing about a real place and can go there to experience it yourself, do it. But know that it's not required. You don't have to go somewhere to be able to write about it well, thanks to the internet. You can learn a *ton* without ever leaving your chair. This is how I've written about a lot of other places.

Street View on Google Maps, while obviously often

outdated, can give you a great feel for your setting. I have used it often to picture myself walking down some random street somewhere, scoping out the perfect location for a setting. If you can't go to the setting for real, it's your next best bet, along with finding someone who has been there to read those parts of the book where you might've messed up.

Once upon a time, I was writing a duet set in New York City, and I needed the couple to go to and from dinner. Of course, I did all the online research to find a great restaurant —sometimes, I use real ones, and sometimes, I create them. Thankfully, at the time, I had someone on my staff who had lived in New York City. She was able to tell me that the route I had the couple take wasn't a good one and that I should instead have them go a different direction, past a certain statue. Well, heck yeah, I took that advice. Anything to make the story more real and authentic—without pulling the reader out of it—is always a plus for me.

There will be times when you get things wrong or things will have changed in that particular real location. It's okay. Do your best. Put the time and effort into your setting to make it as realistic as necessary to add to the story. There is, however, a fine line. If you know a place inside and out, there's always a risk of going overboard and adding so many details that you actually detract from the story. Readers don't need to know every single thing you know in order for your book to be amazing.

Your goal is to make it realistic enough to write an amazing story, not publish a travelogue. Less is more sometimes. Use your judgment and follow your gut.

Setting: Creating Fictional Places

You can also create places straight from your imagination or base them on real places you personally know. I once created a small town in Kentucky where a character was from, and I based the layout and size on my own tiny hometown in West Michigan. To create the name, I borrowed a format from a nearby town and changed a word. I created the characters who populated the town, using my imagination and creative flow. This helped me create a small town that had a vibe that felt truly real, like it was somewhere you could really visit, but it was purely fictional, so I could make up everything however I wanted it to be to suit my story.

You are the god of this world you are creating. Have fun with it. Use your imagination. Borrow bits and pieces from real life and entertainment that you've experienced. It's really not that hard, and the more time and energy you spend on it, the more real and magical it becomes.

You don't have to know every single detail about everything in your fictional world though. That's not the point of the exercise. You just need to know enough to make that world come alive for your readers and to support and enhance the story you're telling them.

Have fun with it! I love creating fictional businesses and subplot storylines that add to the overall depth and richness of the story. Plus, you never know when one of these little setting details you had fun creating can turn into a pivotal part of the storyline. The fictional town you created might end up becoming iconic for readers. That fantasy world you built could end up being where people wish they could truly live.

You have no idea where your imagination can take you. Give it wings and let it fly.

FIVE
PLOTTING

Ahhhh … plotting … one of my most favorite things in life. I absolutely love plotting. It's the time when you can insert yourself into creative flow and let your imagination run wild. If you don't enjoy plotting, writing amazing fiction might not be the best choice of how you spend your time. Sure, you can try to ignore plotting, as some "pure pantsers" do—a pantser is someone who writes by the seat of their pants with little to no plotting—but personally, I don't think that's the best route to take if your goal is to write amazing fiction.

However, I also do not subscribe to the school of plotting your book out in great detail—from start to finish, chapter by chapter, scene by scene—before you start writing.

I can't do it.

It sounds like torture and suffocation to me.

I consider plotting a very interactive and necessary experience, but I don't go overboard. I have to leave room for creative flow to work its magic.

I suppose if I were to be categorized as an author on the

scale of pure pantser to full-blown plotter, I would end up somewhere in the middle. I need to know enough in order to start writing, but not so much that I feel hemmed in and my creativity has no room to breathe.

Every author does it differently. You will ultimately do what works best for you and your process. Hopefully, that process will result in the very best fiction you can possibly write.

Before I start writing a book, I think about it for months, if not years. Literally. I might not write down all the notes, but I have stories percolating in my mind constantly. As I mentioned before, I consider my mind like a stove with many pots on many burners. I might be working on one project, but there are tons of others simmering, marinating, percolating, or being stirred. This is one of the main ways I work effectively with creative flow. I don't worry about what's in the pots. My job is to be receptive to the creative ideas and magic that come to me, often at strange times and in weird places, out of seemingly nowhere. When one of those magical ideas pops into my awareness, I grab it, like a drowning sailor grabs on to a life ring. It might be a thread. A chunk. A piece. A name. An idea. A scene. A thought. A line of dialogue. Or it might be an entire download.

I don't know how many other authors get downloads, but I know that many do. This is one of the coolest things I've ever experienced. You can't predict it, and you can't force it to happen. All you can do is be ready to catch it when it comes and write it all down as fast as you can.

What is a download? It's an energetic packet of information that comes into your energy field from the hand of the Universe itself. For me, because I've been clairaudient for many years, I hear a quiet voice in my mind. It's like a thread. Or perhaps a balloon string. If I grab on to it with my awareness and focus, it keeps pouring information into my mind. Oftentimes, it's a scene or an idea or a character. If it's a character, the character is generally relatively fully formed. It's not just a line or a bit of something or a sliver. It's a sizable chunk of information. It's obviously not the whole story, but it can be an entire scene or the start of a scene with dialogue or a conflict or something bigger than a single line or a vague idea. It's always very specific, and I know it's not coming *from me*, but rather coming *through me*. I don't know where they come from out of the ether. I have no idea when they will come. I just know that they come. And when those downloads do come, I'm always grateful. Then, I try to focus my attention as much as I can on the thread and write it all down so I don't lose it. I follow the thread until it ends, and it often branches off into something else.

To be an author who writes amazing fiction, you always have to be open to ideas, information, lines, scenes, characters, plot twists, et cetera from the Universe. Be aware. Be receptive. When those things come, grab a notebook and pen or your phone and start taking notes. When I get downloads, I write them down verbatim—as fast as I can so I don't miss a single word. The number of plot issues and tricky situations that have been solved quite literally as a gift to me from the Universe is innumerable.

The people around you will get used to it, hopefully. Being an author sometimes means that you have to tear your attention away from whatever or whoever it is on in order to write something down that you definitely won't remember later. And one of the biggest lies authors tell themselves is, "I don't need to write that down. I'll remember it."

More literary goodness has been lost that way than you can possibly imagine.

Grab those ideas. Follow the threads. Write them down. Save them. Use them.

Two minutes can change your entire life, if you take the time to write down those inspired ideas and see where they lead.

I've plotted an entire story in the middle of a concert before, complete with a fully formed hero. The heroine for that particular story didn't come through until a year or so later. I held on to all my notes for *years* before I finally got a chance to write their story. But I had the ideas, both simmering in my head and written down in my notes. That concert ended up being one heck of an investment, and as a result, I ended up with a duet that delighted my readers, scored me two more *USA Today* bestsellers, and made a lot of money.

If your intention is to be open to plot ideas all the time, the Universe will deliver them. Nothing is off-limits. Everything is fodder for your books—your plot, your scenes, and your characters. It doesn't matter if you're waiting in line at the grocery store or sitting in a doctor's exam room. You can think about your story at any time, and great ideas can hit you *anywhere*. Life is an incredible muse.

One of my best ideas came while I was walking down the streets of Barcelona. Another came while on the toilet. Actually, several came while on the toilet.

It's those times when your mind is generally occupied with something completely unrelated to your work that you release all resistance and worry around your story or creative process. Then, creative flow can slip in and drop something *perfect* into your energy field and your mind.

It could come from watching people, eavesdropping on strangers in public, while flying on a plane, in silence while driving—I've sorted through many a plot and book issue while behind the wheel—or really while doing anything.

If you're stuck on your plot and you can't see where to go, take a break. Go do something completely unrelated to writing and plotting, and chances are, your answer will come.

My go-to has always been getting out in nature. Whether it's taking your dog for a walk or sitting on a beach or in a park somewhere, nature seems to help shift the frequency of your being and allow for possibilities to reach you that couldn't have otherwise gotten to you while you were all stressed, staring at a blank page and a blinking cursor.

As you might be starting to realize, writing amazing fiction isn't something you do only a few hours per day while you're in front of your computer with your fingers on your keyboard. As a matter of fact, that's only a tiny fraction of the total commitment needed. Being an author of amazing fiction is something you *are*. You're always that person because your story is always on your mind—or a dozen stories are percolating in the back of your mind—and you're constantly receiving new ideas and interesting tidbits that can help make your books even better.

Also, I think it's extremely important to reiterate that this process is *not linear*. I do not receive downloads and parts of books in any kind of order *at all*. As a matter of fact, oftentimes, I get pieces that I don't even think are related to the same book because they're so different. I don't judge what I receive or the ideas that I have. I just file them away mentally in the appropriate bubbling pot on the stove of my mind or write them down and then see how things unfold.

I've watched magic happen right before my very eyes too many times to question it.

Those pieces that I thought were for different books? At least a dozen times, they have ended up being for the same book, but I just didn't know it yet.

The Divine Storyteller will always feed you what you need to bring your story to life, but it won't necessarily happen the way you expect. That's okay. That's what keeps it interesting.

Often, I only know about the hero or heroine of a story. I don't know who else the story is about. But I keep developing what I do know by mentally stirring the pot—touching it with my attention and giving it some thought energy—until eventually, the rest of the pieces come to me and then come together. At some point, I will know enough to start writing the story.

This is why I spend months or years thinking about characters and plots and stories before I write them. I'm gathering information from the Universe. I'm receiving those invaluable pieces that I could never make up by myself. There's something inside of me that knows when to create and when to wait. It's a part of me that I don't control. It's connected to the deeper rhythms and cycles of life and creation. When it's time to start, I feel it. There's an impatience and an urgency inside me that must be satisfied. That's when I know it's time.

Remember, "Nothing is more powerful than an idea whose time has come." Victor Hugo said that. Amazing stories take time to develop—at least for me. This is how I create real, flawed, layered characters, awesome twists, jaw-dropping cliff-hangers, and epic, memorable romances. I spend a lot of energy and attention on it—often over *years*—before I ever start writing.

It only took me writing one book, whose idea was way too fresh for me, to ever attempt it again. As I mentioned, it was painful and my least favorite book I've ever written. Thankfully, it became a favorite of many of my readers even though I'd almost binned it and refused to publish it.

Moral of the story: Give your books and ideas time to percolate, marinate, and simmer. Just like a meal, that extra time simmering can bring out even richer flavors and subtle tastes that wouldn't have been possible if you'd microwaved it. I'm always after a masterpiece, not a TV dinner.

SIX
THE STRUCTURE OF YOUR STORY

There are a lot of great books out there on story structure and on the hero's journey. I've only written one book according to a "formula," and I didn't love the experience—although I learned a lot and took many pieces of the advice along with me in my writing. As an author who's mostly absorbed story structure via osmosis through reading great books, I'm not the best person to point out the technical parts of what is supposed to come when. I don't actually know. Whenever I'm at some author get-together, it never fails that someone starts talking about what happens in Act I and Act III and how they need to figure out Act II. My eyes completely glaze over. I'm instantly bored. I don't know what Act I is. I don't know what Act II is. I don't care. I write great books without knowing any of that.

What I'm trying to convey here is that you should figure out what works best for you to tell *your* stories. The hero's journey is the most beloved structure by most readers, I believe. It's basically what all movies that people love are based on.

However, I have a confession. I have no idea what the official steps are in the hero's journey, except that I know he has a goal, something is thwarting him (conflict), he wants this goal very badly (motivation), and he sets off to get it (the journey and the story)—and he might have a friend or ally. Setbacks ensue and then a victory of some sort. Finally, we have another big thing happen, then the black moment—when all hope seems lost—and then we have the overcoming of the final obstacle, possibly with the help of the friend or ally, and they all live happily ever after.

That's legitimately all I know about that.

I learned from Dwight V. Swain's must-read book *Techniques of the Selling Writer* that if you want to sell books, you constantly have to increase the tension. Amp it up. Amp it up some more. Then amp it up a little more. Then more. More. More! My books are suspenseful because that's how you keep people in suspense. Tension. Keep bumping that knob up.

Don't be afraid to be mean to your characters. They don't need you to protect them from everything. Going through hard stuff makes everyone stronger, and it'll make your characters stronger too. Don't make it too easy on them. Get them to dig deep and truly transform into the person they could always be, but without the conflict you introduced, they might never have risen to the occasion to fulfill their destiny.

Besides, no fiction reader wants to read a book that has nothing interesting happening and no transformation of any character or circumstances at all.

Life is a fascinating story, and the Universe is the ultimate storyteller.

I constantly say, "No one would believe that if I put it in a book," about true things that people have told me or that I've personally experienced.

Life is always inching up the tension. It's how we learn and grow. If we were never under pressure, we'd never step outside our comfort zones. It's part of evolution. So is your story. A lot of people on this planet want to watch someone triumph against all odds to live happily ever after with their true love. After all, it's what a lot of people on this planet personally want to experience. If they can't get it in real life, they'll get it from books or some other source.

Keep your structure interesting.

If you need more guidance on structure specifics, I highly recommend James Scott Bell's *Write Your Novel from the Middle* and *Super Structure*. Also, do yourself a *massive* and *potentially life-changing* favor and read Dwight V. Swain's *Techniques of the Selling Writer* if you want to sell books. His advice has been invaluable to me and my career.

Why I Don't Use Beat Sheets or Other Writing Structure Aids

I don't know what a beat is. I said this to my former editor over lunch many times, and every single time she tried to explain it to me, I swear, my brain would just shut off. I didn't want to know. I didn't want to understand. I don't think like that, and my mind has no interest in adapting to that terminology.

As mentioned earlier, I also don't know what acts are or use those when I write. I don't use any particular structure or formula either. I don't like formulas. I like freedom. The freedom to create whatever I want is important to me, and I feel hemmed in by other people's methods because they reduce the amount of freedom I have to create.

However, in the beginning, I tried a lot of things. I even tried beat sheets once upon a time, when I was working on my second book, but I felt like I was trying to shove a square peg in a round hole. I'm not a cookie-cutter writer. I don't know how to fit my creative process into a box. Use whatever training wheels you need to get the job done, but be aware that you can always change, adjust, evolve, and grow—and you should! Growth is great!

Start as Late as Possible; End as Early as Possible

I think this was one of Elmore Leonard's top 10 tips for writing that, once upon a time, I read on Alessandra Torre's website, but I might be misremembering. If I'm wrong, I have no idea where I learned this, but I think it's great advice.

Start your book as late in the action as possible. End it as early as possible.

Start your chapter as late in the scene as possible. End it as early as possible.

Why?

Because you want to keep your book moving. Pacing is very important. You want to keep it exciting. You want to keep it riveting. Starting in the middle of the scene, after all the boring setup other authors might write, is a great way to do that. What do I mean exactly by this in practice?

Let's say I have a chapter I want to write. The scene is happening over the kitchen table at dinner and includes a shocking announcement. I can start the chapter in lots of different places. I can start the scene while someone is setting the table, while everyone is being seated, during the small talk, after everyone starts eating the meal, during dessert, et cetera.

There are a lot of choices to be made in every single book. How do you figure out where the best place to start the scene is? I go for the spot that will have the most emotional impact and provides the most exciting opening to the chapter. I would probably start the scene with the shocking announcement. No intro. No explanation. I'd just hit the reader with the big guns first.

For example:

Chapter 7

"Jacqueline is having my baby, and we're getting married."

The clinking silverware and the murmurs of small talk went silent instantly, as though a conductor had halted an orchestra. Mother's fork clattered to the china as she stared at me in horror, unaware of the arugula caught between her teeth. Every head swung as if on a swivel, mouths gaping first at me and then at Jacqueline.

Well, this was going fabulously.

I just made that scene up on the spot. If I were writing this scene, I would drop the bomb, play up the drama and the reaction, bust out some snappy and impactful dialogue, make the point I came to make, and then I would get out of the room and scene as fast as possible before heading to the next chapter. That might sound quick and like I'm leaving a lot of other stuff out of the scene, but you don't have to show the reader everything that happens from the beginning to the end of the meal. It doesn't matter who set the table or who clears the table. That's not important here. Keeping your readers engaged in the story and turning pages as fast as they can *is important here.*

Chapters don't need to be a certain length. They just need to be good. A reader has no idea how many words a chapter has in it. They don't know how many words the book has in it. They don't care. They just want the best story. Getting in and out of scenes quickly can make them pop and really add excitement and interest to the book.

However, know that this is a rule of thumb. This doesn't mean that every scene should feel like the beginning and ending got hacked off with a machete. You have to feel your way into it and through it. If it feels choppy, smooth it out later. *Everything is fixable.*

Amazing fiction is created one amazing scene at a time, each one building on the last. You don't want anything in your final product to feel choppy. The book needs to flow. But it should also be as interesting as you can make it. Starting late and ending early is a great way to keep scenes interesting. It also stops you from including a ton of setup that readers have to wade through to get to the good part.

I could have started my imaginary scene above with

dinner conversation, passing the butter, everyone eating and enjoying a meal, or six dozen other different ways. But the point of the scene was for our mystery man to drop the bomb on his family that he's marrying someone at the table who they didn't know he'd knocked up. That's the interesting part of the scene. I would suggest delivering that interesting information in a way that's going to be the most memorable and exciting. Rev up the drama by dropping the bomb with some shock value. It won't just be Mother in the scene with arugula in her teeth who remembers it. Readers will too.

Original, But Not Too Original

If I wanted to make my readers ecstatic, I would write almost the exact same stories I've already written, but I would make them different. Readers want the same story as the story they already love, but different. I know that might sound odd, but it's true. Readers don't want wholesale, brand-new, absolutely-different-in-every-way stories. They just don't. They want what they love, but they want it to be different from what they've already read. Think about it: when you finish an *incredible* book, you basically want to read another book just like it, but different. It's why a lot of readers will devour an author's entire backlist. They're looking for the same feeling, but different characters, storyline, conflict, et cetera.

When I set out to write something I thought no one had ever written before, I managed to do it. It was tough, especially because it was my very first book, but I did it. It was a postapocalyptic ménage. No, for real. It was. Then, I published it.

It turns out, maybe there weren't a lot of postapocalyptic ménage stories out there because people weren't into it. Maybe it was *too* original. Granted, the 17 people who read it upon release *really loved it* and even wanted a sequel. But the market in general, at that particular time, not really. It didn't generate much interest.

Spotify found out about this phenomenon of people wanting new, but not altogether new when they were sending out lists of new songs to subscribers, according to a book I listened to, called *Hit Makers*. They accidentally included some not-new songs in what was supposed to be a totally new playlist. When they discovered it, they sent out a list of all new songs, never heard before, and people weren't as excited about this revamped list as they had been about the list that included old favorites *and* new tunes. It turned out that people needed some old stuff and new stuff together for the best results, which Spotify had found out completely by accident.

If you've never written a book before, it's easy to think that you should write something completely and totally original. Something that is *nothing* like anything you've ever read before. It seems logical to think that's the route you should take. However, this might not be the path most likely to take you to success.

In all honesty, I don't worry about it anymore. I just write the story that I'm most excited about and most in love with at the present moment. If I love the story, then someone else is going to love the story too. I don't worry about how original it is, or if someone else has done this type of thing before, or if this character has a feel about him or her that's similar to another character I've already written. I write the story I love. It turns out, I love a little bit of old with my new stuff too. Don't worry about trying to be 100% original. It's not worth your concern. As long as you're not deliberately copying someone, what you write is going to be different because *you* are different and this is the first time you've ever written it.

How Long Should Chapters Be?

Chapters should only be as long as necessary. I know there are people out there who say every chapter should be 2,000 words or something like that, but I disagree completely.

I have chapters over 4,000 words and even some as short as 11 words. It's all about what works best for the story and what will have the most impact on the reader. That 11-worded chapter I wrote? Totally memorable and impactful. Also totally worth it. Learn the rules and then break them.

Let the chapter tell you how long it needs to be. Don't worry about living up to someone else's idea of perfection. That's irrelevant to you writing amazing fiction. Feel it out. Make it as long as it needs to be and no longer. End it on a mini cliff-hanger if you want that suspenseful, emotional impact. Then, move on to your next awesome chapter. Don't overthink it. Just go with what feels right to you in the moment. If it doesn't read well when you reread the story, then fix it in rewrites.

Finally, don't let anyone tell you what you "have to do" as an author. This is your world. Your universe. Your creation. Do whatever feels right to *you*. And if this is your first book, then realize that you've got a lot of learning to do. It's okay. We all start out having written *zero* books in this lifetime. That's how this works. No one comes into this as a pro out of the gate. We all learn by doing. Give yourself grace and get the words down.

How Long Should the Book Be?

When you start a new story, one of the first things your mind is going to ask you is, *How long is this book going to be?* Or in my case, my mind asks, *How many books is this going to be?* It's right up there with, *Can I actually do this?*

Here's the short, honest answer: it doesn't matter. It doesn't matter how long the book is going to be. It doesn't matter how many words or books it will take to tell a story. What matters is how good the story is, not how many words it takes for it to be told.

If you ask my beloved husband, Jake—the man who has lived with me through writing over 30 books and has been part of my creative team every step of the way—he'll tell you, "It will take as many words as it's going to take." And that's the gospel truth.

Unless you're writing for a publisher who has given you a specific word count for your story or you're playing games with getting paid per page or for some other reason in the self-publishing world, word count is the last thing that matters. A good story takes as many words as it takes.

Do you think readers care how many words Harry Potter is? Or how many books it took for J.K. Rowling to bring the entire story to life? No. They care about the story. They care about getting lost in the magic. They care that it *exists* for them to read. It's not the word count that matters.

Don't get hung up on making your book a certain number of words. Yes, books of certain genres are traditionally and historically certain lengths, but with the advent of self-publishing, a lot of traditional and historical rules went out the window. At the end of the day, readers care about reading a great story. If you give that to them, they generally only have one complaint about length—they always wish it were longer.

That's a longing you'll never be able to satisfy completely, if you do your job. Always leave them wanting more.

And jumping back to the question that often floats through all of our minds: *Can I actually do this?* The answer is yes. Yes, you can. Yes, you can, if you believe you can.

Even after nearly 40 fiction titles, the thought still surfaces in my mind. *Can I? Do I know how to do this?*

My answer to that thought these days is always an *emphatic yes*. It always works out. I always figure it out. The story always comes together. It's just a matter of time, patience, putting in the energy and effort, and having faith. Faith in creative flow, faith in the process, and faith in yourself are essential parts to writing amazing fiction.

SEVEN
ALMOST READY TO TELL THE STORY

What I Need to Know to Start Writing a Book

Since my second book, I've had a mental checklist of the big things I usually need to know and have plotted out—for the most part—for every story before I begin writing, although there are exceptions to every rule.

These are things I spend a lot of time thinking about and must know before I ever type the words *chapter one*:

- *Deep dives into character development.* I need to have a really good grasp of who my characters are before I can start, and I need to create GMC charts for each of the main characters. It will still take me at least 10,000 to 20,000 words or more to really understand them and learn who they are in action, but I can't start a new book until I know a lot about the main characters. I need to know who they are, what they want, why they want it, and their unique personality quirks and characteristics. I need to know who I am being when I put myself into their shoes and live life through their eyes and experience what they're experiencing. I can't write the character without *being* the character, and I can't be the character unless I know the character well.

- *Big plot points.* I need to know how the book starts, the first scene or first few scenes, and the worst thing that will happen to the characters during the course of the story. I call it the "black moment." You can call it whatever you want, but it's that moment when all hope seems lost and the hero or heroine has been thwarted to such an extent that it feels like there's no way to overcome the challenge. I've only written one book—my first—without knowing the black moment, and it made it very difficult because I had no idea where I was heading with the story. The story meandered here and there, from scene to scene, with no discernible direction in mind. Knowing the worst thing that is going to happen to the characters gives me a great idea of where I'm heading, and generally, I know how the book is going to end after that black moment. I also like to know a few big scenes throughout the story. Big moments that are going to be turning points or exciting. I love those. I often know many of them in advance. It helps me write faster and more efficiently if I know several scenes sprinkled throughout the story because it gives me a bit of a roadmap for the journey. I might know A, B, C, J, P, W, and Y. I don't need to know every scene though. Those populate along the way for me and take me on some wild adventures I didn't see coming.

- *The setting.* I need to know where the story is taking place and the main locations where the characters will be. Knowing this in advance allows me to make the setting more realistic and colorful and doesn't slow me down while I'm writing. I have to know where I am while I'm living as the character. I have to know where I'm walking around. What I'm touching. What I'm smelling. What I'm seeing. What I'm feeling. Without those important setting details, the story won't be as impactful, realistic, and engaging.

- *Names.* I need to know character names or at least have a list of names handy that I can pull from to name characters who pop up. For me, there's nothing more annoying while writing than not knowing what to call a brand-new character who just appeared and trying to slap a name on them in the moment and having it feel wrong. It pulls me out of creative flow because it doesn't feel right and makes further writing challenging. Naming characters in advance, as well as having a list of names handy for surprise characters, leads to better writing sessions for me. I also like to know the names of the major places in the story. As I mentioned, I greatly enjoy creating fictional businesses as part of my books. It's very fun for me, and the more interesting the places are in the story, the more memorable they are for readers.

That's mostly everything I need to know before I start writing. Everything else, I figure out as I go.

I love plotting while I'm writing. Some authors need to know everything in advance before they start writing—every chapter, every scene, every moment. That's awesome for them, but it sounds horrible to me. It feels like there's no room for magic to happen and everything is too well planned out to allow for sufficient creativity and surprise. I *love* being surprised by my characters and the events in my stories. It's honestly one of my very favorite parts of the creative process. I love when I didn't see something coming and I'm totally shocked by how it plays out. That's the coolest! Why? Because I know readers are going to be totally shocked too. This is an emotional experience for them. Keep it interesting!

If you're bored by chapter three, because you've already done all the fun, creative work up front and you're now just slogging away to get your story on paper, I truly believe the energy of boredom will come through in your work. If there's still some mystery and you don't have everything figured out, then it's highly likely you'll keep your readers guessing along the way too.

I don't know about you, but as a reader, I love to be shocked and surprised and to gasp out loud. I don't want a book to feel predictable. If I can already tell what's going to happen with the storyline, why should I bother to spend my precious time reading it? Sure, there are some readers who *love* predictable fiction. They love that formulaic *wash, rinse, repeat* style of writing. That's wonderful. There are plenty of authors who love to write that kind of fiction. It's easier, from what I hear, and it can be quite lucrative.

But not for all the money in the world could I make myself write like that. I'd be bored on the first day and have a new job by day two. Every author is different. As I've stated multiple times, I'm a hard-core reader first. I write for myself. I create work that I love. It isn't for everyone, and that's fine. There are tons of authors in the world and millions of books to choose from at every given moment. Readers gravitate to what they like. Neither you nor I can make every reader happy. We're not supposed to. We're supposed to write the best books we possibly can and offer them to the world to see what happens next. My kind of books sell really well. It turns out that there is quite a market for shocking twists, jaw-dropping cliff-hangers, amazingly layered characters, epic romances, and storylines that grab hold of you and don't let you go until the very last word.

However, I think it's important to point out that I didn't set out to write a specific kind of book. The style of book I write happened organically, as a result of me learning what I liked as a reader and learning what I could produce as an author. I just kept trying to do better and better with each story. My goal has only ever been continuous improvement—making each book better than the last.

I can report back to you now that it has been a winning strategy for many, many years. I have no regrets, and I'll keep writing books this way until I, my processes, and my creations evolve. We are each a unique creature. Our creations will be just as unique as we are. It's a beautiful process and one that gets even more efficient with time.

Tenses and Point of View

Before you start writing, you have to decide what tense you're going to write your book in and from which point of view. It'll be past or present tense, most likely, and either first-person or third-person point of view. Ultimately, only you can decide how you want to write the story, and at some point, the decision must be made so you can start writing.

I started off writing in past tense from the third-person point of view. If you don't know what that means, it's writing about things that already happened in the past and told from the point of view of the character whose head you are in, but not from the "I" of the character. It's being told *about* the character.

For instance: *Jack didn't know his head could pound like a freight train, but when he opened his eyes and the light seared his pupils, he knew last night had not gone according to plan.*

A first-person point of view would be through Jack's eyes: *I didn't know my head could pound like a freight train, but when I opened my eyes and the light seared my pupils, I knew last night had not gone according to plan.*

Arguably, a deep, well-written third-person point of view will give the reader the same emotional experience as a first-person point of view. At least, if it's well done.

Writing in the past tense from third-person point of view used to be the most common and most traditional. Then, the indie publishing revolution happened, and first-person, present-tense storytelling became very popular.

Once upon a time, I wouldn't read books written from the first-person point of view in present tense. I hated them. It felt amateur to me after decades of reading thousands of books written in third-person and past tense. Often, it felt too painful to me as a reader because of the insane conflict and emotional trauma wrought by many an early indie author. However, as they always do, things change.

I fell in love with reading stories from the first-person point of view in present tense. Eventually, I switched to writing in first-person and present tense for many of my stories. I felt like I could take the reader deeper into the experience of the story by using that combination.

However, you have to make this decision for each story that you write. I don't think there's a one-size-fits-all approach unless you're an author who can only write a story one way. I believe that for me to be a great author, I have to be able to write in present or past tense and in first-person or third-person point of view—and do it well. However, many authors will write in the same tense and from the same point of view for every book they ever write. I choose what will serve the story best. Also, when I was writing many, many stories back-to-back-to-back, I would switch tenses from series to series to keep myself challenged and interested in the actual writing itself.

When does first-person point of view make the most sense? I think that first person makes the most sense when you're planning to experience the entire story through one character's point of view or from two characters' points of view. This can create a very fun, immersive, emotional, entertaining experience for your readers.

When does third-person point of view make more sense? Possibly when you're creating a story that will be told through the experiences of many people. However, you have to be much more aware and vigilant about not head-hopping—jumping in and out of different characters' heads within one scene without a demarcation or some sort of indicator of change for the reader (something that was popular in older fiction for a while and it worked for them). If you head-hop too often, you can confuse your reader. They might not know whose point of view they are supposed to be experiencing the action through. You get better at writing "in character" as you gain experience though, and it becomes easier for the reader to seamlessly slide from one person's point of view to another's when you're writing in third person through the use of your word choice and characterization.

I'm currently still figuring out how to tell a story I've been thinking about for ages. I want to write it in first person, but I have many characters whose point of view might be used during the story, and I haven't decided if I'm going to try to pull off a multicharacter first-person point-of-view story when, normally, I would only use first person for a single or dual point-of-view story. Ultimately, I'll choose whatever is in the best interest of the story and the way I think I can tell the story best.

Tense and point of view are really important decisions that you have to make up front about how you're going to tell the story. Pick whichever will enable you to create the best experience for your readers.

Ultimately, doing what you're good at is great. But going outside your comfort zone when the story calls for it is also wildly important. Don't be afraid to stretch your creative wings and try something new. Yes, it might be challenging. Yes, it might be hard at first. But you'll get used to it eventually, and writing in your non-preferred or non-usual style might actually end up being just as easy as what you're used to doing right now.

Stretching your wings and pushing your creative boundaries is healthy for an artist. Don't avoid learning new things and new methods. Elevating your process and your creativity can lead to stunning creations you didn't know you could create. Sometimes, you'll even impress yourself.

Pro tip: I do not recommend writing two books in different tenses at the same time. It's *painful*. I once was writing two different stories at the same time, doing morning and afternoon shifts. I was trying to write in past tense in the morning and then present tense in the afternoon. What happened was that I would mess up both of them and spend the first hour of my writing session getting back into the correct tense that I was supposed to be in already. It was a giant pain. It sucked. I ended up putting one story aside and focusing on the other because it was just too hard on my brain to write efficiently in two different tenses every day.

A final word on point of view and tenses: If you are writing a series, keep the point of view and tense of your series the same. Don't switch it up from book to book, if you can possibly help it. Readers like consistency and continuity in these even if they don't realize it. The last thing you want is to write an amazing second book in a series and have your readers feel like something is off about it because you switched from past tense to present tense or from first person to third person. Write the whole series the same way. Switch it up when you start a new series.

Also, you can start a new series anytime. You don't have to finish one before you start another. There are no rules here really. We're all just making things up as we go.

Recognizing the Need to Make Space

I took a three-year break from writing fiction once upon a time. I had to. I was burned out, to a crisp, and I couldn't keep going forward. I had run my creative well so dry that the very thought of writing another story had me breaking down in tears. As a matter of fact, any thought of work related to being an author had the same effect. It wasn't a fun time in my life, but it was necessary.

That break was revitalizing and amazing. I learned all sorts of things during that time that I couldn't have learned while I was using every single bit of my energy for plotting, writing, and launching six to nine books per year. As you can imagine, that took a lot out of me, and I wasn't properly caring for myself to restore my energy levels and refill my creative well on a daily basis. I was more of a *go until you can't go anymore* kind of author.

All of this is backstory to explain how and why I know so intimately the necessary requirements to dive back into writing amazing fiction. As I'm sure you've guessed, writing amazing fiction takes a lot of energy and focus.

During my break from writing fiction, I filled up my life

with all sorts of other energy-consuming habits, tasks, and responsibilities. Things I *never* would have undertaken while writing because I would never have been able to think about doing those things while my mind was full of juggling six or more storylines at a time on top of running a multimillion-dollar publishing company.

But give me some free time, and I will fill it with all sorts of things.

I never expected it would be *so dang hard* to get back to writing books. It took me months of frustration, wanting *desperately* to start a new book, but somehow, I just couldn't.

I wanted to. I had a lot of the story mostly figured out. But I couldn't.

Why? Because I had not created enough space in my life to allow the process to begin and unfold.

For me, writing amazing fiction takes a *ton* of energy, focus, available mental space, and uninterrupted solitude. I recognize now that without all four of those conditions being present, I can't work my magic.

When I was writing six to nine books per year, I was rabidly territorial about my time. I didn't allow anyone or anything to creep into my life and take up the time that I needed for writing or thinking about my books. My boundaries were 100-foot-tall concrete walls. Writing time and plotting time were sacred.

But when you take three years off and are available so much more to people and for new projects and new ideas, all those boundaries get eroded.

The people who wouldn't think of bothering me for any reason at all during my sacrosanct writing hours were suddenly able to talk to me mostly whenever they needed. They loved it, and I loved it—until I wanted to go back to writing.

It took me months to figure out that in order to go back to writing the amazing fiction that I loved to create so that the world could experience the magic that existed in my mind at all times, I had to create space in my life.

I had to wind down projects. I had to slim down staffing. I had to shut down operations on a business I'd started in the meantime. I had to erect massive boundaries around my time again—not just with other people, but also with *myself*.

Basically, I had to make writing the book so important in my world that I would be moved to make changes in my daily life that would eliminate distractions and interruptions, create uninterrupted blocks of time for creative solitude, and give myself the space I needed to be wildly creative.

I couldn't do that at the same time that I was running six companies and working with six people on a daily basis. It didn't leave me enough mental, creative, physical, or emotional energy or space to bring an amazing story to life.

Eventually, I sorted out the changes I needed to make—with the help of a big kick in the butt by the Universe—so I could get back to writing.

Never again will I ever discount how much space is required in my life and in my mind to write amazing fiction. It isn't something I can just squeeze into a few minutes here or there.

My stories are so all-consuming that I couldn't even begin to think about writing one until I had the appropriate amount of space in my life and had freed up all the necessary energy.

So, I got empty. I emptied out my mind of all the other concerns that had taken up residence in the past three years. I let go of my goals and any thoughts about the future. We stopped trying to do so much. All so I could write again.

This journey that I'm on has never been easy. Writing amazing fiction requires a lot of sacrifice, discipline, and determination. You have to want this so badly that you're willing to do whatever it takes, including implementing wholesale lifestyle changes, in order to get where you need to be.

It's not something you can simply do for the money. Chasing only the money will burn you out—and quickly. It has to go deeper than that if you want it to be sustainable. For me, at least right now, I'm writing amazing fiction because I can't *not* do it.

The story in my mind that's coming to life on the pages is so amazing that I can't *not* write it. *I want to read it desperately. So desperately that I wish it were already done so I could read it and experience it.* But I'm the one who has to do the work and write it. I owe that much to the Universe who gifted me with this amazing idea. I owe it to the world because they'll never get to experience this incredible story until I do my part—which is a lot of hard work. Mostly, I'm doing it because the thought of not writing it and letting the idea go to someone else is too unfathomable to allow it to be reality.

Once I created enough space in my life, I could finally sink into the magic of creative flow and remember why I'd started writing in the first place. Because creative self-expression is part of who I am and what I came here to do.

Don't ever underestimate or downplay how incredible it is to write an amazing fictional work. It is *incredible*. It is a feat. It is a ton of hard work. It takes a massive amount of energy, focus, commitment, discipline, and determination.

Give yourself the space you need in your life to do it. Don't beat yourself up if you can't focus on your book because the rest of your life is just too nuts or too busy. This too shall pass.

And if bringing your story to life matters enough to you and you want it bad enough, you'll find a way. Magic always does.

Getting Help Versus Creating in a Silo

I don't know many successful authors who create in a silo without any input or feedback from anyone during their creative process, and I know *a lot* of successful authors.

I also don't create in a silo. I always need help. I have people who help me every single step of the way when I'm writing and publishing a new book.

And while getting help can be extremely useful and important, you have to know what kind of help you need so you don't end up asking for help from people who will ultimately derail or take away from your creative process.

First things first. You must develop creative boundaries and be able to enforce them. *You* are the final say. This is *your story*. You are the god when it comes to your book. It doesn't matter what anyone else says. *You make the final decision.*

How do you do that? I don't know if it came naturally to me in creative territory, but while I struggled for *years* to learn to set any other kind of personal boundary, setting creative boundaries has never been hard for me.

This is my story. I do whatever is in the best interest of the story. I don't care if it's my idea or someone else's idea. I don't care if I have to cut 40,000 words or add three new chapters. At the end of the day, the only thing I care about is publishing the best story I can possibly create in that moment. Whatever that takes, it takes. It's not easy, but it's not impossible when I keep my focus on what is best for the story. *I serve the story*.

As you can maybe tell, I have no ego about these things. I can't have one. Ego around my work would pervert creative flow, and I would never end up with the best book I possibly could.

I want the best ideas, wherever they come from, to grace the pages of my books. That means I have to recognize that I don't always have the right answer. Sometimes, there's a question or issue or plot point that I just can't figure out. Sometimes, I think about it and come up with a big blank. Or I might know A, C, F and X, Y, Z, but I don't know how to connect the dots to create an actual book that anyone would want to read.

While I deal with this situation in multiple ways, one of the best is seeking help. I firmly believe that every author needs a trusted sounding board, where you can share your creative ideas without feeling stupid—or too stupid—and can get input from someone with a different perspective, different life experiences, and access to a different set of options in creative flow.

If you don't have someone in your life who can do that for

you for free—like your partner, a friend, a colleague, another author, or someone else—then you can always hire someone to fill that role. For years, I worked daily with a developmental editor while I was writing. I did this because there was a point in time when I didn't have anyone in my personal life who could fill the role for me, and I also didn't have the time or energy necessary to trade critiques with another author. I was writing too many books in too short of a time frame to be able to critique someone else's work fairly and effectively. Paying someone meant that I didn't have to feel guilty about needing their time and effort when it was convenient for me. There are a lot of other pitfalls and potholes that you can wind up in if you take this route, but you can definitely make it work for you—if you find the right person.

At the end of the day, whoever you work with during your creative process has to be the *right person for you*. Beware of energy vampires and people who want to feel important because they worked on your book. Also, beware of people who act like the story is suddenly theirs. It's not. Their opinion is not more important than yours. You're the author. What you say goes. *Always*. You're doing the real hard work of bringing this creation into being, no matter how much help you get. Don't let someone bully you during your creative process because many people will if you let them.

I still prefer daily feedback on my writing when I'm in full-on fiction drafting mode. I like to know that what I think is good is actually good and that the story feels like it's still heading in the right direction. Could I write without that? Absolutely. But eventually, I will have to get feedback and constructive criticism because I recognize that I'm too close to the creative process to see my work clearly. You often need an outsider's opinion to get a solid sense of where you are.

Plus, creative types love to assume that everything we create is crap. I made that assumption about my own work for years. I would assume everything I wrote was garbage until someone told me it was good. I don't take that approach anymore. I actually know that I'm a great writer now, but even I need a lot of feedback so I can make the story the best it can possibly be. After all, that's the only reason we're doing this—to create the best story we possibly can and let it loose in the world to be experienced by others. As far as I can tell, that's extremely hard to do if you're writing in a silo. But, if that works for you—great!

Get the help you need, whenever you need it, as part of your process and don't ever feel bad for needing help. *Every* successful author I know has a trusted sounding board for plotting. *Every single one.* Find yours. Be grateful for their time, effort, and creativity and try not to be too harsh when you reject their ideas that don't fit with your vision of the story.

Get Comfortable with Uncertainty

You only need to know what you need to know when you need to know it. That's the honest truth.

I only know bits and pieces, scattered throughout the entire story, at first. I know this one guy seems bad, but he'll end up somehow being good later. I know there's a prophecy that's super important, but I have no idea what the prophecy actually is. I know it seems like this character is dead, but later, he'll show up somewhere else, adding tons of drama and impact.

Writing amazing fiction means that you don't know everything at once. It's an adventure. You know what you know, and then you work with creative flow or talk it out with someone to figure out more. Then, you go write some scenes, and more of the blanks will get filled in as you write. Or you get shocked and surprised and some crazy, new wrinkle is thrown into the mix.

Writing amazing fiction is an interactive, creative process. You don't know everything that's going to happen in the story. You have to be comfortable with not knowing exactly what is going to happen. Instead, focus on the pieces you do know with total certainty and confidence and build from there. The rest of the book fills itself in as you need it to. I'm not saying the story writes itself exactly, but almost. *Almost.* You still have to do the work and spend the time thinking about it and plotting and discussing it with someone, but the story will shape itself and take you on an amazing adventure with it, if you let it.

I truly believe not knowing everything up front is a key to writing amazing fiction. Getting comfortable with uncertainty and not knowing everything that is going to happen will allow you much more flexibility and creativity in your drafting. You can do magical storytelling acrobatics within those unknown spaces.

I never know exactly how my books are going to turn out. I just know they're going to turn out. As long as it's *awesome*, then I did my job. It doesn't matter that the best scene is one whose idea wasn't mine or that the shocking twist seemed to have come straight from the ether without me expecting it. Every amazing book is a win regardless of how it comes about.

Check your fears, self-doubt, and ego at the door. Leave space for magic. Then, allow yourself to write it with the help of creative flow.

EIGHT
CULTIVATING CREATIVE CONFIDENCE

Cultivating creative confidence can be a lifelong process. It's not linear, but it is worthwhile to continually work at it.

What is creative confidence? Your belief that your ideas are good and worth putting the time and effort into in order to translate them into form rather than leaving them in your mind or the ether. Creative confidence means that you don't think your ideas are stupid and better left unexpressed.

In order to successfully write a book and publish it, you have to have quite a bit of creative confidence. You have to believe that your idea is awesome. You have to believe in yourself and your vision. You have to believe that you can bring it to life.

If you've never written a book before, that might seem like a big jump, but you can totally get there. Dedication, patience, effort, and self-belief will literally take you everywhere in life, including down the road to becoming a successful published author.

How do you know if your ideas are good? I feel my way through mine.

Again, this is where solitude and silence are key in my process. I think about my ideas and options, and I picture them. Whichever idea or option gives me the most excitement and *hell yes* feeling is the one I go with. If it feels kind of *meh*, I keep hunting for something better.

No one but you will be able to tell if you think an idea is awesome. It's only your heart and your body that can communicate with you in this intuitive, instinctual way.

Yes, you can run your ideas by other people to see if they're good, but be cautious before you embark on that journey.

Sharing your ideas with the wrong person—or even the right person too early—can take what might be an amazing idea and shred your confidence about it, causing you to abandon it.

Once upon a time, I was working out a twist for a book, and I was sure that I had *nailed it*. My idea was *epic*. At the time, the only person I was really sharing my ideas with on a daily basis was my law firm secretary. She was an amazing help and super supportive. She basically loved every idea I'd ever brought to her. But for some reason, this idea did not click with her.

She didn't get it. She couldn't see it. She didn't like it.

Talk about a blow to my creative confidence.

I was pretty devastated, to be honest.

But instead of tossing my idea out the window, I went on a road trip to meet up with a friend who was part of the "book world" and ended up talking my idea out with her. I'll never forget sitting in her SUV, getting gas at Costco outside of Chicago, explaining this twist idea that I had for my story.

She got it. She loved it. She told me to go for it.

I went for it.

That ended up being my breakout book. No one saw that twist coming, I don't think. It was my first really good twist—three books into my author career.

I'm so grateful I didn't give up hope about the idea when the first person I shared it with didn't get it. I'm so glad I stayed true to what felt like the right thing for the story despite the fact that the person who loved everything I'd written up to that point didn't like it.

Have confidence in your ideas, especially when you *feel* that they're really good. I know it's hard for a lot of us to acknowledge our creative genius because of the societal programming around us that doesn't like us to get "too big for our britches." But we really are amazing and capable of incredible works of art.

Why shouldn't we have creative confidence? It makes creating easier. It makes it more enjoyable.

You don't have to be a tortured artist. You can be a happy one. That comes with believing in yourself, no matter what and regardless of what anyone else says to you. That kind of strength might not come easily to some, but it can absolutely be built up.

Be patient with yourself. When your heart tells you that your idea is amazing, believe it. When your ego tells you an idea is amazing, question it. If you can't tell the difference, start figuring it out.

The heart speaks quietly—in feelings, intuitions, and

instinct. The ego is often very excitable and loves being superior and impressing others. Getting to know the difference between what part of you is speaking will change your life and improve your decision-making on every level. Plus, your writing will get better.

Just like in life, the quality of the choices you make in your book will determine how awesome the book is. Once you decide to go a certain route, stop second-guessing yourself. I think of it like the general rule of thumb when buying a wedding dress. Once you've picked it out and bought it, you stop looking. I treat each choice in my books that way. Yes, there are an *infinite* number of ways your story could go. It's up to you to pick the one that feels the best and leads to the best reader experience and story outcome. Once you pick, move on to the next choice. Don't waste your time thinking about what could have been if you'd gone a different route. Unless, of course, that route is superior and you're willing to do all the work to go back and change your book to take it down a different road.

I follow my excitement and my *hell yes* feelings. So far, they haven't led me wrong.

Finding Your Voice

Finding your voice as an author can be tricky, especially when you're just starting out. You don't know what you sound like as a writer. That's okay. You'll figure it out.

Before I first started writing, I read a lot of other books—somewhere in the neighborhood of 10,000 to 15,000 over the course of my life. I knew what I liked. I knew whose voices I connected with the most. When I started writing my own books, I naturally emulated the voices of those authors whose work I loved and respected. I didn't *copy them* per se, but I tried to sound somewhat like them. I guarantee you, there are people out there who started writing their first book by emulating my voice. That's okay. I don't care. I think it's awesome and an honor.

But the most important thing about being an author is to find your own voice. You have a unique voice. We all do. You don't need to sound exactly like your favorite author to be successful. As a matter of fact, I truly believe that by finding your own voice, you find your own success. Besides, if you're constantly imitating someone else, you're never leaving room to become the original, unique, amazing talent that *you are*. Who cares if your books don't sound the same as anyone else's? You are not anyone else. You're you. You're the only you that will ever be. That's incredible! Be yourself! Be original!

It will take time and probably several books before your voice becomes clear. That's okay. It's a process. Over time, you will distill your essence, and it will shine through so brightly in your work that the people who know you will know that only you could have written it.

That's why I have no problem sharing all my secrets that I've learned and the processes I've never told anyone about. I finally realized that even if I gave all my secrets and tools away to the world, it didn't mean anyone else could write exactly like me. Because they're not *me*. That's the essential ingredient in my work—*me*.

I'm the only one who has had my life experiences. I'm the

only one who sees the world through this particular lens. My consciousness is totally and completely unique. It cannot be replicated, and therefore, my work cannot be replicated. Copied and imitated, sure. But no one else can write like me the way I can write like me. Because I'm the only me. My voice will always be *my voice*. And what's more, it will change. It already has—many times. Because I have changed. My books are not the same because I am not the same.

As a matter of fact, you can watch me change through my books if you know where to look. My essence comes through my characters, and what they're going through is sometimes what I'm going through. I laugh all the time because my first two books were about heroines who wanted to run away from their lives—which was exactly what I wanted to do at the time when I was writing them. When I realized I couldn't only write contemporary romance for the rest of my life, the heroine in the book I was working on suddenly wanted a new job. Just like I did. My last published fiction story included a heroine who literally left her life behind and started a new one with her soul mate. Which was what I was dreaming of doing at the time.

Your voice isn't just how you write. It's what comes through your characters. There is so much of you in your stories, if you are self-aware enough to see it. I wasn't always that self-aware. It wasn't until after the fact that I started realizing I could see my changing mindset and desires in my characters—playing out under different circumstances, of course, but it was still there.

I once wrote a book, my only romance about a couple that

was already together, when I was struggling with how to make my relationship work with my insane workaholic tendencies. I worked that out in fiction before I worked it out in my real life.

No one can steal my voice because no one else has lived my life. Let yourself be authentic in your writing. Be naked. Bury it under layers of fiction. Most people will never know, but your books will probably get better.

And if you fear that you'll never find your own voice, stop worrying about it and just write. It'll come through naturally. You don't even have to think about it really. One day, you'll just realize that your books sound like you in a way that no one else's does. And then, *bam*, you're there.

Giving Yourself Permission to Suck

Before you start drafting your book, there is one step that I find to be absolutely invaluable. *You have to give yourself permission to suck.* Accept the fact that it is perfectly okay if your first draft sucks. It might sound weird, but I find it to be imperative.

Once upon a time, I literally wrote myself a permission slip and stuck it next to my monitor when I was really struggling with getting going on a new book. My permission slip said something like this: *This might not be the best book I've ever written, but it's the best book I can write right now, and that's okay.* I kept that permission slip near my computer for years. I needed to know that it was okay if I sucked.

Being an author of commercial fiction is not the easiest

path one can take through life. And despite what some might think, when you get super popular and even world-famous, it doesn't get any easier. In fact, it only gets harder. All of a sudden, there are tens or hundreds of thousands or even millions of people who have a vested interest in what you create. That's *a lot* of pressure. There have definitely been points in my career when I have buckled under that pressure. Hence, my permission slip.

It's okay to suck. It's okay if your first draft sucks. It's okay if your first book sucks. It's okay. Give yourself permission simply to *create* without all the added pressure. And remember, no one is going to read that crappy first draft unless you let them. It can be absolutely awful. You have no idea how terrible some authors' first drafts are. *Horrendous.* And I'm talking about authors who make *a lot* of money from writing books.

Give yourself permission to get the story down in whatever form and fashion necessary in your first draft. It doesn't matter if you think they're the worst words you've ever written or that there's no way on God's green earth that they could be turned into something readable or saleable. That's not important in the beginning. What's important is getting words on the page.

Nora Roberts, author extraordinaire, offers us another one of my very favorite writing quotes because of its absolute simplicity and brilliance: "You can't edit a blank page."

If you're so worried about making your first draft perfect, you're probably going to spend a lot of time staring at a blank page. That's not useful when you want to have a career writing fiction that pays not only your bills, but also allows you to live the life of your dreams.

You have to get the words down. It doesn't matter if they're good or not. Only words on a page can be edited. Only words on a page can be fixed.

I only say this because I've lived it.

I've lived with the crippling fear of demanding perfection from myself too many times. I know how hard it can be to give yourself permission to suck so you can just move forward with the story.

If I don't give myself permission to suck, I tend to throw away a lot more words because I'm trying *too hard*.

You're going to have more than one draft. The quickest way to get to that second draft is to stop beating yourself up about your first draft and just freaking write it.

Easier said than done, I know, but it is possible.

Moving Beyond Fear

I know we've already talked a little about fear, but it's something that keeps coming up when you're living a creative life. Fear isn't exactly your enemy, but it's definitely not your friend either. One thing I've learned is that what people often fear the most is what other people think—especially when it comes to allowing other people to see them look stupid or fail. It's not the looking stupid or failure itself that's the hardest part—at least in my experience—but it's knowing that other people are seeing it happen. Living a creative life means that, sometimes, your creations won't hit the way you hope and shoot to the moon the second you release them out into the world. That's okay. It happens. Not every creation is meant to find a massive audience. It doesn't make them any less incredible or amazing.

To move beyond fear, I firmly believe you must stop caring what other people think about you and what you're doing. Caring about what other people think is a trap and something to work out of your system as soon as humanly possible. But because you are human—presumably—it can be very tricky. We're programmed by society to place high value on other people's opinions, but how much value is there really? No one else knows what is in your heart. No one else has to understand or approve of what you're doing or why you're doing it in order for you to become massively successful at it and completely change your life. I know because I've lived it.

The best advice I can offer on this subject of moving beyond fear is something I learned through my personal experience: Don't tell anyone else what you're doing. Keep it a secret.

Or at least, don't tell *everyone* what you're doing. It makes it *so much easier* to chase your dreams and take those big chances and huge risks and really *go for it* when you don't have a giant audience waiting to see how everything you do turns out. It's a lot less awkward to have your first two books flop when no one really knows that you're even publishing them. It's a lot harder when you have a book flop and you know *lots of other people* are watching. I've lived that too. It sucked. It wasn't fun. But you do become stronger as a result. Everything serves in its own way after all.

Still, if you can possibly manage to keep your big dreams

a secret, you will be doing yourself a giant favor. I did this when I was first starting out. I told my close friends and some family that I was going to become a successful full-time author, just like the ones I had read about in *The Naked Truth about Self-Publishing*, making *bank*, but I only told four of my coworkers at the big law firm where I worked.

I don't know about you, but I didn't show up in this life as a great secret keeper. A vault I was not. At least, not until I started letting my creativity thrive in the real world, which resulted in me living a double life. I wasn't technically even allowed to publish my first book while working at the law firm where I'd been a corporate associate for seven years. They had a no-moonlighting policy, and I was supposed to get permission from the Management Committee if I was going to earn an income from any source other than the law firm. Let's just say, I'm more of an *ask forgiveness* rather than *ask permission* kind of person. I broke their rules, and I didn't care.

It actually turned out to be a great choice. Not because my first book was a massive success, but because it *wasn't*. It was so much less awkward to release a postapocalyptic ménage romance novel that totally flopped when no one really knew I was even doing it. And when my second book flopped, there was really no one asking those awkward questions about how my release was going and if I had become the successful self-published author I'd said I would become.

Having those awkward conversations—about why your dream isn't coming true yet—is not helpful in my experience. It sucks to talk about your failures while you're in the middle of them. It's not fun to admit that your big dreams haven't materialized yet. And from a *law of attraction* standpoint, talking about why they haven't come true seems to be a big ingredient in pushing them farther away from you.

But still, I maintain that the best reason to keep it all a secret, as much as you possibly can, is because it makes it so much easier to try new things. If you don't have a bunch of people waiting with bated breath to ask you how it's going when things aren't going well, you can cruise through those tough times and keep your focus exactly where it belongs—on the goal.

For me, almost every fear around writing that has come up isn't actually fear about the writing itself at all. It's a fear about what other people will think. Don't let other people's potential opinions stop you from writing the book of your heart. It doesn't matter if they approve or disapprove. That's not why they're here. Each one of us is on this planet to live our own life to the fullest. For many of us, that means we're here to take these stories inside of us and get them onto the page and out into the world for the masses to read.

If I hadn't been brave enough to fail multiple times, I would never have made it to success. Keeping what I was doing a secret made that so much easier. The world doesn't need to know every single step you're taking. The world doesn't need to know about every moment you live and every thought you have. Keep some things to yourself and show the world what you did when your masterpiece is complete. And you don't even have to tell them then.

I didn't tell anyone anything for years, even after I was majorly successful by every measure. Keeping it a secret from people in real life became a habit I didn't break for many years. I only broke the habit because Jake was so proud of me that he'd told everyone who I was, what I wrote, and that I was a best-selling author.

I remember asking him why he had to tell everyone my pen name and all about my books.

He just looked at me like I was the slow kid in class and told me, "Because I'm so freaking proud that I want everyone to know my wife is a rock star."

How could I argue with that?

Bottom line: Your fears aren't helping you. Any fear that is keeping you from writing the words in your heart and soul or doing the things you dream of doing is actually keeping you from living the life you were born to live.

Fear and self-doubt are two doors we all must walk through. It's not unique to you or me. We've all heard it: everything you want is on the other side of fear. *It's true.* Fear is the mirage. Your dreams becoming reality and the life you can't even imagine living because it's so wildly incredible are both on the other side of your fears.

Everyone has to overcome each of their fears in their own way, in their own time. You're not too late. You haven't missed out. Life is waiting for you to get up the gumption to do these things that you've been thinking and dreaming about doing for so long. It will all happen in perfect timing, if you can just face the fear and walk straight through it.

Write in secret. It works. Don't tell everyone what you're doing. Publish in secret, if you want. Tell perfect strangers all about what you're doing if you need to get it out. You can live a double life if necessary. I did it for years. I'm not saying it's the only choice or even the right choice, but it's a possibility, and it worked like magic for me.

Do whatever you need to do for you to get past the fear and get on to writing your amazing fiction and living the life of your dreams.

PART TWO

DRAFTING

NINE
DOING THE WORK

One of the first things many new authors ask me is what software program I use to write my books. I guess I shouldn't be surprised because I wondered what "real authors" used, too, when I was writing my first book on an iPad with one of those crappy magnetic keyboards. I didn't want to write it on my work laptop, and that was the only computer I had that functioned at the time.

Long story short: You can write a book on any word processing program and any device that you have access to. You can even handwrite a book. There are people who actually still do that.

I use plain vanilla Microsoft Word. I tried Scrivener once upon a time, which many people love, but it slowed me down. It seemed to have too many bells and whistles and was too complicated for the contemporary romance I was writing at the time. However, I can see how those extra bells and whistles could be really useful if you're writing something that's more complex, like fantasy or science fiction. I've even considered using it for my fantasy project, but I don't know if I want to take the time to learn a new program. Efficiency is key for me, and if changing my process requires mastering a brand-new learning curve, I often prefer to get on with the writing part instead. However, if you've got some procrastination time free, that would be a perfect use for it.

There are other writing software programs out there, even some that I've heard can create some kind of story structure for you. At this point in my career, with 39 fiction titles under my belt, I don't want a software program telling me how to structure my fiction. But if you're a newbie, it could be helpful. However, beware of relying too heavily on any one tool to write your stories. You want to help yourself grow as a writer and as a creative, not ride a bike with training wheels your whole life. Although, whatever helps you helps you. Writing a book is hard work. Use whatever you need to get to those magical words *The End*.

Spoiler Alert: The Book Won't Write Itself

Just like all spoilers, I know that's a super bummer to hear, but it's true. Sometimes, it might feel like the book writes itself—which is fantastic—but you still have to do the work.

I was so burned out after writing 39 books that I used to dream and fantasize that if I just thought hard enough about it, I'd open my computer one day, and there'd be a fully written book, ready to rock. Those were the fantasies of a burned-out writer, and they didn't come true *exactly*.

Writing books is work, but if you love it, it's some of the

most worthwhile work possible in which to invest your time and energy.

Why? Here's one major reason that should not be overlooked: when you write a book, you do the work once, and then you get paid for that work *forever*. How many other jobs are there like that? This is one of the reasons I find writing books to be one of the best vocations there is, but perhaps that's because, less than a decade ago, I was a lawyer, selling my life away six minutes at a time to clients. You only get to bill the hours you work. Just like most people only get paid for those hours they actually spend working.

Not so when you're an author. I took three years off from writing fiction and kept getting paid the big bucks because I had done years' worth of work that were still paying out. So, when you're thinking about how much you don't want to sit down and write, remember that this is work that could potentially still be paying you in 20 years or even longer. And what's even better is that you can take the work you did once, and you can turn it into multiple streams of income. You can turn your manuscript into an audiobook. You can have it translated into other languages. You can even sell the film rights. This is why it's worthwhile to put in the time up front and write amazing books. Amazing books can become your retirement. And what's more, if you get a reputation for writing amazing books and you build a good-sized audience, anytime you need a cash infusion, you can write another book. No one can put a limit on how much money you can make. Not your boss, not the economy, not anyone. You can be recession-proof and self-sufficient. That, my friends, is freedom. At least for me, it has been.

Writing amazing fiction is an excellent investment of your time if it's something you already want to do. If you're simply doing it for the money, it's going to be a lot harder and more painful. Having a passion for storytelling and writing makes it much less so.

But above all, you have to *believe you can do it.* You have to believe you can write this book. You have to believe your dreams are possible for you. Then, you do the work. Invest your energy and attention into something that has the potential to change the rest of your life in a multitude of positive ways.

But first, we have to do the work. So, let's get to it.

The Beginning Matters the Most

We've all heard the saying, *You get one chance to make a great first impression.* It's never truer than with the first page of your book. There are millions of choices for entertainment out there, so you have to hook your reader quickly. Immediately even. Right now, attention spans are shorter than ever before. Think of how long a video clip holds your attention before you scroll onward. Do you give it 10 seconds? Think about how popular short videos are on TikTok. Social media has done authors no favors with the attention span of readers—or listeners, in the case of audio.

What does this all mean? The first 250 words of your book are absolutely vital. They are more important now than ever before. You have to nail them. You have to hook someone fast and well and keep them hooked. I call it "grabbing the reader by the throat and dragging them through every single page." That's why so many of my reviews call my books "unputdownable." Because I write books that readers finish. Not the ones they DNF.

With that being said, you need to stop worrying about the pressure of nailing these first 250 words. Instead, begin thinking about the best starting point for your story.

How do you pick a starting point? A lot of authors opt for a prologue. I, however, rarely write prologues. They're too easy to mess up unless you have a solid purpose and solid execution. If you can pull off a prologue in a way that hooks the reader and brings them into the main body of the story, where you can drag them through every single page, then great! Do it. But make sure you have a purpose and a strategy —and an incredibly well-written prologue. Remember, on page one of your book, the reader doesn't care about your characters yet. It takes time to build a connection between the characters and the reader.

Instead, I prefer to start with one of the following: a shocking event, a shocking statement, a whimsical statement, a hilarious statement, or an intentionally fascinating but confusing WTF moment.

As you can tell, I prefer to grab the reader's attention *immediately* by making them feel something. Shock. Curiosity. Humor. Amazement. Awe. Wonder. Confusion.

Your job, as an author, is to play with the emotions of your reader. Weave them into the story. People *never forget* how you make them feel.

Regardless of whether you start with a prologue or a regular chapter, you have to make the beginning of your story interesting. Your storytelling starts immediately on page one. Your job, as an author writing amazing fiction, is to write books that will enthrall readers. Books they won't want to put down. Sure, there are moments of rest necessary in books, points where the storyline eases back a bit on the pressure, but those moments should be strategic, and in my opinion, they should never be on page one.

Any moment where the reader has a chance to put the book down is a moment where you are gambling on if they will pick it back up again. I don't know about you, but I'm not much of a gambler. I like to go for the sure thing. And one thing I know for sure is that if a book isn't memorable, especially from page one, a reader might never finish it. It's essential to write stories that keep the reader engaged in every scene in order to have a high read-through rate, which translates into a successful career. Writing books people finish is the most important thing an author can do. And that starts with an amazing first page. Grab them. Don't let them go until you hit *The End.* That is a story well told.

Make your reader feel something. Connect them to the story immediately, if possible.

Pro tip: Beware of the urge to data-dump on page one. Data-dumping is what I call dumping a character's entire story or backstory in the first chapter. Remember, *readers don't care about the character yet.* They're not emotionally invested in the story yet. Don't waste your amazing backstory and golden character nuggets in the early pages when the readers don't care. At that point, it just feels like a slog through information that isn't yet relevant to them.

I think there's some rule of thumb that you shouldn't divulge a character's backstory for the first 10 pages of a book or something like that. I can't remember the rule exactly, but I feel like it's a reasonable one. However, I do agree that rules are meant to be broken. But I am also a huge proponent of learning the rules first *before* breaking them. They generally have a reason for existing. Backstory and background information should be doled out sparingly, especially in the beginning of the book.

First, we hook them. We get them invested or curious or at least interested in what's coming next. Then, we move into exactly what's unfolding. I favor bold first scenes. Shocking moments. Whimsical juxtapositions. Ridiculous situations. But even I break my own rules and start with something else occasionally. It all depends on what is in the best interest of the story. Spend time thinking about the best place to start. Spend time thinking about the most interesting first scene you could possibly write in this story. Put yourself in the shoes of your reader. What is going to hook you and keep you turning pages?

Until I have an epic first scene, I won't even consider starting to write a book. Not just any scene will do for your first. It has to be *awesome*. It has to kick-start this amazing story, grab the reader's attention, and *keep it.* The reader has to *feel something* as a result of that first scene. *What* they feel isn't nearly as important. They just need to feel *something* that will keep them reading.

Grab them on page one—in the first sentence. Bring them along through the whole first paragraph, first page, and first chapter. *Do not let them stop reading.* Lead them by the hand to the next scene—or drag them by the throat, if you prefer. This is your job as an author. If your first page doesn't grab a reader and they never make it to page two or chapter two, you haven't done your job.

Another pro tip: Don't make your first 250 words or your first chapter too complicated or too bogged down with details. Keep the length of your descriptions reasonable. Don't overload your reader with stuff they don't care about. Beware of too many adverbs and adjectives. Again, learn the rules and *then* break them if you want. Keep your writing tight and crisp for maximum impact. You have a short window to capture someone's attention and keep it. Take that window seriously. It matters a *ton*.

I, personally, have one of the highest DNF rates in reading fiction these days. Life is too short to read boring books. There are tons of places you can focus your attention that will be more interesting or riveting.

If I want entertainment in the form of fiction, I want to be engaged. I want to be hooked. I want you to drag me through every single page. I want to feel compelled to keep reading—or I won't. I'll find something else.

Every reader has their own threshold of interest and window of opportunity. You're gambling on how long that is with the beginning of your book. Make it count. Engage readers in a big way.

My own personal rule of thumb is that I never write descriptions that I would skim as a reader. And guess what. I don't love tons of descriptions as a reader. This is my personal preference, but it also means that my books aren't overly detailed in the description category. I'm an old-school reader who wants room for my imagination to fill in the blanks. I want to watch a movie in my head and see something pleasing to me. My own tendencies as a reader greatly influence how I write my own books. After reading over more than 10,000 fiction stories, I prefer to keep things interesting and well paced. But at the end of the day, it's most important that *you like your story*. Write what *you like*. Write what keeps *you hooked.* You're the first reader. If you don't like it or you think it's boring, change it. That's what rewrites are for.

And trust me, don't worry too much about nailing the writing on this scene in your first draft. Do your best, of course, but know that this will be the *most rewritten scene* in probably almost every single book. You want your first scene to shine. It has to if you want your book to be a success. After you've finished your first draft and before you send that book off to edits, rewrite and self-edit it until it's the best first scene you could possibly write in that moment. After you've done your absolute best, rest easy and keep going. You've done everything in your power to make it awesome, and that's all anyone—including yourself—can ever ask of you.

Ending Chapters on a Cliff-Hanger

I mentioned this briefly before, but ending your chapters on a mini cliff-hanger is such a fun writing method that it deserves further discussion. It is absolutely one of the best ways to keep your readers on edge and flipping pages furiously. I learned this from many a Sidney Sheldon novel 20-plus years ago.

I love suspense. I love the feeling of not being able to put a book down because the story is *so good* that you just *have to know* what happens next.

Ending your chapters on a mini cliff-hanger makes this easier to pull off as an author. Readers and authors alike have asked me many, many times how I do it.

I don't even really think about it anymore. It comes very naturally to me. If I can leave the reader hanging in a suspenseful fashion at the end of a chapter, you'd better believe I'm going to do it if it makes the story better.

Writing in dual point of view makes this really easy, in my opinion. Basically, all you have to do is end the chapter on a suspenseful note—getting out of the scene as early as possible is useful for this—and then start a new chapter from the point of view of the other character, especially if they happen not to be in the same place at the time.

Readers can't wait to get back to the point of view they just left because they desperately want to know what's happening to that character too.

Also, another important point: when you end a chapter on a cliff-hanger, you don't always have to know what's going to happen after your mini cliff-hanger. I often don't know what's going to happen next. I make that up as I go. It keeps my readers guessing because they don't know either. How could they know where the story is going if I don't? It generally works out great for everyone, providing a memorable, entertaining experience.

Show, Don't Tell

If you've been a writer for more than five minutes, you've probably heard this advice. You might have also wondered what it really means. What is showing? What is telling?

Showing is living the scene as your character. Telling is explaining to the reader what's happening.

I prefer to write books that a reader can experience, like a movie playing in their head. That requires a lot of showing—basically, putting the reader in the character's head and moving the reader through the story so they can watch it and experience it through the character's eyes.

The best way to learn how to show, in my opinion, is to write with your eyes closed. Literally. See the scene in your mind's eye. *You are your character*. What are they experiencing? Feel it as though you are the character. Relay what you're feeling, seeing, and perceiving—the sensations, smells, sounds, emotions, bodily reactions, and so much more —onto the page, as if the character is experiencing it firsthand.

Here's an example of showing that I'm literally making up as I go:

Thud. Thud. Thud. The pounding in my skull drags me through the fog of sleep into consciousness. *Ugh. What did I do? Why does my head hurt so much?*

I stretch my jaw from side to side, hoping it'll help relieve the pressure, but it doesn't work.

Thud. Thud.

Gingerly, I open one eye, only to slam it shut again. *Oh, man. Too bright.*

Where am I? What happened last night?

Showing is you writing the experience like it's happening to you personally. You're the character. You're experiencing what the character is experiencing. Your job is to translate that into words in such a way that the reader can slip right into that character's mind and body and live the experience as the character too. This is why knowing your characters so well that you can *be them* is important.

Here's an example of the same scene through telling:

I woke up, and the light was too bright. It hurt my eyes, so I closed them. My head was pounding, but I didn't know why. What happened last night?

In this example, you're the character *telling* the reader what is happening to you. You're not giving them a chance to experience it firsthand. It lacks the interest and emotional impact of showing.

As far as I understand it, that's the difference between showing and telling. Showing tends to have a lot more emotional impact because the reader is experiencing what the character is experiencing right along with them. That means the reader is enmeshed in the story. They're no longer holding a book and existing separately from the story. They've become part of the story, and outside reality has ceased to exist. That's awesome. That's the experience amazing fiction gives a reader.

But, like all rules, there are always reasons to break this *show, don't tell* rule too. I use telling in my books often. There are certain scenes and moments that don't need to be shown for whatever reason. Perhaps it's boring and it would bog down the pace of the story. Perhaps it's just stuff you need to get through to set up another scene. You absolutely can use telling, but you have to know where, when, and how. I don't have a good rule of thumb for that. I just write and let it come. If it doesn't give me the feels I need when I'm rereading the manuscript, I fix it in rewrites. After all, *everything is fixable*.

However, if you're not in love with your story or your characters, I can see how it would be very easy to slip into telling during the story where you should be showing. If you don't love the story or the characters, it's hard to want to *be them* and experience the storyline as it is happening to them so your readers can have an immersive and amazing experience as well.

The work you're doing in showing is purely to create an incredible reader experience, which is one of the hallmarks of writing amazing fiction.

Show where you need to show. Show where you need emotional impact. Show where you want reality to disappear and readers to become one with your characters, experiencing the storyline as if they were your characters.

Tell where you need to tell. Tell when you need to move things along and jump from one point to the next. Tell when it feels like you're sharing something that readers don't need to experience firsthand because it's not adding to the immersive reading experience.

At the end of the day, you're the god of this world you're creating. You're creating an experience for others to have. You get to do whatever you want, which can be slightly terrifying because of all those incredible possibilities out there. Learn the rules. Then, break them as needed.

Welcome to being a creative artist. It's really the best vocation there is, but I'm certainly biased.

Pacing

Pacing is key to reader engagement and the story being read all the way to *The End*. You need to bring the reader along on this journey. You're not just telling them a story. You're walking them through an experience.

Why the distinction? Because when you give a reader an experience, you're impacting their entire biochemistry and their personal electromagnetic field. You're changing them. You're making them feel things. You are the conductor for their orchestra of emotions. You're evoking emotion with maximum impact through your own unique voice and writing style. A well-paced novel includes a constant ratcheting up of tension. As I mentioned before, I learned this from Dwight V. Swain, in his 1965 classic, *Techniques of the Selling Writer.* I highly recommend you read it. It was life-changing for me.

Hook them on page one, then ratchet up the tension. This will determine your pacing. Use your intuition to feel out the best emotional flow for the story. Feel the events of the plot as you translate them into words on the page.

If you can't connect with the emotions in your own writing, figure out how.

Writing amazing fiction means that you must feel your way through it. You must travel the same road that your reader will travel. If you feel nothing, what are the chances the reader will feel nothing?

Remember that Robert Frost quote? "No tears in the writer, no tears in the reader. No surprise in the writer, no surprise in the reader." I mention it twice because I believe this is the absolute truth, and I have lived it many, many times.

I am shocked at points during every story I write. That's the fun part for me. Readers are *also* shocked. I believe that's a fun part for them too. When tears are streaming down my face while I'm writing, which happens often, there's a really good chance that readers are also going to feel super emotional during that part of the story.

An amazing fiction writer feels the story first and keeps it moving along, inching up the tension and the stakes as they continue through the plot. This is how a story turns out to be well paced. It keeps moving. It isn't bogged down. It doesn't lose steam.

Keep it interesting and immersive, and your readers will follow you anywhere you want to take them.

Dialogue

Amazing fiction requires great dialogue. Read your dialogue out loud. It should sound conversational. If it sounds stupid when you read it out loud, like a conversation no two people in real life would ever have, then edit it until it sounds like a conversation people might actually have in real life—regardless of the subject matter. Dialogue should sound natural. It shouldn't sound dumb or contrived. No one likes that. Also, resist the temptation to constantly use character names in the dialogue. You'll do it more in fiction than people do in real life, but don't overdo it.

If you find yourself struggling with dialogue, become a

student of your life. Pay attention to the interesting conversations you have with people.

In fiction, you don't need all the setup and endings that you do in real life. You don't need every conversation to start with a greeting that takes seven lines and ends with a good-bye that takes half of a page. But dialogue in fiction should feel natural and not forced. Above all, it should sound reasonable when read aloud. And if you think everything you write sounds stupid when you read it aloud, practice being kinder to yourself. You'll get better. You can always edit and rewrite.

I love good dialogue. I love snappy, fun, fresh dialogue that keeps a scene moving and the pace clipping along. It's interesting, and it's awesome. It also fills up pages quickly.

Beware, however, of an easy rookie mistake when it comes to dialogue—using a ton of unique dialogue tags.

Trust me, I wanted to do this so badly when I first started writing fiction.

For some reason, it can be easy to think that *he said* or *she said* is too boring for your book. You might be tempted to write *he quipped* or *he intoned or he said acerbically.* However, as impressive as your use of unique dialogue tags might potentially be, you can't get away with too many of those instances in amazing fiction.

Said, asked, and *replied* are the basics, and you will see them repeated in books over and over and over again until kingdom come. Why? Because they disappear in the eyes of the reader. Readers don't notice *said, asked,* and *replied.* They basically blend in with the dialogue. They're expected. They're what every other book uses over and over again.

It's when you start getting into those creative dialogue tags that readers start noticing them. I'll never forget that Jamie McGuire's monster hit *Beautiful Disaster* used "said acerbically" twice. It stood out to me on the fabulous audiobook, but *only* because I'd just read Stephen King's *On Writing*, where he tells you that you should never use an adverb with a dialogue tag. *Said*, *asked*, and *replied* disappear. No one remembers how many times you used *said* in a book. Tack something else onto it though, and readers might start remembering your dialogue tags instead of just the amazing story you're telling them.

Again, this is another rule you can break when it seems right to you. But be aware and use unique dialogue tags purposefully if you're going to use them.

Another way to tackle the subject of dialogue tags without using *said*, *asked*, and *replied* is to show with body language or physical action who is doing the talking. You can use gestures as well. Perfecting this method can be a lifelong journey in your writing as you avoid being too repetitive by using the same movements and descriptions too often. This is a place where your creativity can truly shine even if no one ever really understands how much work you put in on this point. Oftentimes, readers won't appreciate those details, but they will appreciate how well the dialogue flows and how effortless it feels to read the story.

Raising the Stakes

Dwight V. Swain is the master at explaining how and when to raise the stakes, but I will share my thoughts on the topic regardless.

When writing amazing fiction, you must constantly up the stakes. As I've said repeatedly, you have to ratchet up the tension. Yes, there are moments when everyone is having fun and not everything is going to hell in a handbasket, but those moments should be strategic. Your hero is on a journey. That journey can't be easy. An easy hero's journey is boring. Life is too short to read boring books.

Keep amping up the conflict and tension, little by little, one scene at a time. The characters should face setbacks, unexpected difficulties, and complications. I add this stuff as I go with most of it arising organically out of creative flow and the circumstances of the plot. Feel your way through it. There's no formula for when to increase the tension effectively in your particular story. It's something you have to feel and do as you write.

If the heroine has three options to get her out of a tough situation, block off two of those exits and remove the quick and easy possibilities. This effectively leaves her with only one option that points her in the direction you want her and the plot to go.

It's not mean. It's necessary.

Your characters should have to overcome hardships, challenges, and adversity. The harder, more challenging, and more adverse the circumstances are, the stronger the character will become through these exertions, and the more the character will transform. The transformation of the character is important. Readers want to see it. Give it to them. Make it awesome by ratcheting up the tension throughout the story and seeing how the character reacts, adapts, and overcomes or fails. Eventually, you're going to raise the stakes so high that the character probably will fail to overcome something, and that's okay. Actually, that's great. That's part of the hero's journey. The character will have to find more resources, dig even deeper, and try even harder to achieve their goal—which makes for amazing fiction.

Effective Storytelling

The job of an effective storyteller is to take the amazing movie-like production in your mind and translate it to paper. Put yourself in the shoes of the character and see the world through his or her eyes.

What do you see? What do you feel? What can you hear? What temperature is it? What does it smell like? What does your intuition tell you? What is the voice in your head saying? What do you perceive? What do your instincts say?

The goal is to get the reader to watch your story like a movie in their own mind. Your job, as the author, is to write it so well and so engrossingly that they can do that easily.

This is why pulling the reader out of a story is something I avoid at all costs. It's like cutting the power to the movie theater in the middle of the movie—you lose all the suspense and tension you've worked so hard to add. It's jarring, and you run the risk that the reader might put the book down and never pick it back up again. Don't do that to your readers if you can help it.

TEN
GETTING THE WORDS DOWN

As you probably realize, the most important part of writing books is actually writing them. It's quite simple in theory but sometimes much more difficult to do in practice. That's okay. It's normal. You're not the first writer who has had trouble getting the words down. It's a marathon, not a sprint.

But there are ways to get words down that are extremely helpful, and one of them *is* to sprint.

When I first heard about sprinting, I literally thought writers were talking about going outside, lacing up their running shoes, and running as fast as they could. I was a total newbie once too.

In the writing world, however, sprinting is timed writing with the goal of writing the most words you can get down during a specific period of time.

In the world of professional authors, sprinting is often used and with great success.

When I was really struggling to finish my third book—

which would ultimately become my breakout novel and give me a career—a sprinting party changed everything for me.

A bookish PR company had formed a Facebook group for a write-in, I think they called it.

Basically, a bunch of authors were in the group, and a PR person would make a post that said something like, "Go! Write as much as you can for the next 30 minutes!"

We'd all get off Facebook, open our documents, and type as fast as we could until the 30 minutes were up. Then, we'd hop back on Facebook and comment with how many words we'd managed to get down during that time period.

Sprinting creates urgency, which is great because your attention is engaged and fully focused on the task at hand. That's ultimately the most important part about getting those awesome words down while writing—complete engagement of your attention and total focus. That's when you can get caught up in creative flow and thousands of words can pour out of you in a very short period of time. It's awesome. And for me, that particular experience was life-changing.

Throughout the years, I've sprinted with lots of other authors. Sometimes, it's through a messaging app or text messages. It doesn't really matter how you do it. It's kind of like having a workout buddy to keep you accountable. I'm pretty sure that's why it works.

Someone else knows you are writing at the same time they are, and you're both trying to write as many words as you can during the designated time period. Many of my books were written completely through sprinting. It works.

How long is a good length of time to sprint? That depends

on what feels best for you. It could also change as you give it a go.

I've sprinted for 15 minutes, 20 minutes, 30 minutes, and an hour. For many years, 15 to 30 minutes was a sweet spot for me. I could easily knock out 500 words in 15 minutes or 1,000 or more in 30. When you apply total focus, concentration, and maximum effort, *magic happens*. Words pour out of you that you never could have written under different circumstances.

However, you don't have to have another person writing at the same time as you in order for sprinting to work. As long as you can apply total focus, concentration, and maximum effort during your sprinting session, you're golden. But writing with a buddy can be awesome too.

Many authors also love to use the Pomodoro method of sprinting. It breaks up sprints into a series with short breaks, followed by a longer break, then more sprints and breaks. Some authors write all of their books using various sprinting methods because it's an easier way to get your butt in the seat and your hands on the keyboard, determined to get some words under your belt and move your characters down the road of your plot.

They even make apps for this type of focused concentration. You can download a Pomodoro timer app if that's your jam. And, of course, they make apps for your self-control that will lock you out of everything on your computer other than your Word document, if you wish. Back when I was introduced to sprinting, many authors employed an app on their computers called SelfControl. You could also block yourself from being able to access specific websites, like social media platforms, instead of the entire internet, so you can still research as needed on the fly.

Our world is *filled* with distractions. There are a million other things you could be doing or thinking about that have nothing to do with your book. And once the shine of your new, amazing idea has worn off and you're about 40,000 words into an expected 80,000-word novel with a deadline looming, you might have to find ways to keep yourself focused and on the straight and narrow.

Sprinting and an accountability buddy can totally help.

However, be wary of pushing yourself too hard or beating yourself up if you aren't rocking out major word counts. Every person and every day are different. Above all, always be kind to yourself. Treating yourself poorly will not improve your writing or your productivity. It mostly just makes you feel bad about yourself, and then your creativity suffers along with your productivity and your self-esteem.

My first book took me nearly two years to write. I had no idea what I was doing despite having read over 10,000 fiction novels. As I discovered, that didn't mean I knew how to write one. I had to do a lot of research, learning, and procrastinating before I finally figured it out.

My second book took me six weeks to write. It wasn't that I suddenly *knew* how to write a book because I'd done it once. I actually felt like I had no idea how to do it. But there is one reason it only took six weeks, however. I figured out key scenes and my characters' goals, motivation, and conflict before I started writing, *and* I worked on the book every single day until it was finished. I set a daily word count goal, and I didn't stop writing every single day until I hit it.

If you commit to writing 1,000 words in your story every single day and you're shooting for an 80,000-word book, you'll have a book in less than three months. Isn't that awesome? Small, consistent progress can often be better than knocking out 10,000 words in a day and then not knowing what to write for days or weeks afterward. Or in my case, feeling like you can't write for days afterward because you blew so much energy at one time and pushed yourself too hard.

I don't go for massive word counts every day, but if you are trying to get books written and are consistent about how long it takes you, setting a daily word count goal is great. Only you can decide what that word count goal will be for you. Also, know that it will likely change over time.

I started with 2,000 words per day, then moved to 2,500; 4,000; 5,000; 6,000; and then 8,000—when I was feeling really ambitious and under a ton of deadline pressure. I've had many a 10,000-word day and even written over 12,000 words in a day. I once wrote 35,000 words in a three-day weekend to finish a book. This is what I can tell you from my experience: More is not always better. More does not always lead to better quality. My rewrites on the books where I wrote the biggest chunks the fastest were probably some of the most painful.

My best advice for finding a good-feeling word count goal is to write as much as you are able to write day after day, still producing great material and not running yourself completely dry every day on ideas. I like to stop my writing sessions for the day while still knowing what's going to happen next. If I write all the way until I have nothing but blank walls in my mind and I have no idea what is going to happen next in the plot, it can make the next day more difficult or even cause me to skip a day of writing to figure it out. That big word count day is ultimately not the most productive writing session if it causes me to lose a day later. That's what I discovered about writing 10,000 words per day. It wasn't sustainable for me. Yes, I wrote books *really fast*, but I was often so exhausted the next day that I didn't want to write; plus, I had to do tons of rewrites later.

Writing and creating amazing fiction demands a huge amount of energy. You might not feel like you're doing much because you're just sitting in front of a computer and typing, but that's not the truth of the matter. You are using *a lot* of energy—mentally, emotionally, physically, and spiritually. This is why you can feel totally *meh* or exhausted after you finish writing for the day. Writing is extremely energy intensive, even though you're not doing manual, physical labor, Remember that and set your goals accordingly. Having energy left over to live and enjoy the rest of your life is really important in the long run, although sometimes, it can feel less important in the short term.

I lived my life like my books were the most important thing in the world. Everything rose and fell in my world based on how the book was going. Ultimately, that was a destructive way to live for me. It took a massive toll on my physical, mental, emotional, and spiritual health as well as on all my relationships. If you are focusing all your energy on writing and creating, there's not much left to go around for everything and everyone else. Be aware. Make good choices about how you spend your time, energy, and attention. Only you can decide what the best balance is for you and your life.

And again, always keep in mind that just because you *can* doesn't mean you *should*.

Trust me, I know exactly how tempting it is when you start doing the math and realize you can write a book in eight days if you can just knock out 8,000 or 10,000 words per day. I've done it. I did it back-to-back-to-back with no breaks in between for one of my trilogies. I drafted each book in about a week. The fallout nearly killed me. I don't recommend it. However, I did what I did, learned what I learned, and I didn't die. At this point, I count the wisdom I gained from my experience as the ultimate win.

Never forget, *you are precious*. You deserve your own care. The better you can balance your creativity and writing with taking care of your body, mind, and soul, the longer you will be able to produce amazing fiction. Don't be a burnout story. There's already plenty of those, myself included.

The Least Frustrating Way I've Found to Write

How do you come up with 8,000 or 10,000 words of stuff to write in a day, some of you might be asking? Let alone, how do you do it every single day?

Did I mention this *writing amazing fiction* thing takes tons of time, energy, commitment, and determination? I wasn't joking.

I can pretty easily and consistently write 2,000 to 2,500 words of fiction per hour. I can keep up this pace for several hours with breaks in between. What I learned from doing this daily for years and years is that for every hour I write, it takes at least an hour of thinking and plotting time to know what to write. So, even if I was only writing 4,000 words per day during a two-hour writing session—which is an easy, joyful pace for me—I was working on my books a lot more than two hours per day. I was thinking about them often, making lots of notes in my journal or on my phone, and spending at least an hour per day discussing the plot with whoever was my plotting partner at the time. So, all told, writing 4,000 words each day required a time commitment of at least four to six hours, depending on where I was in the story, how complicated and complex it was, and how many corners I'd written myself into.

I learned pretty early on that the most frustrating days of writing were those days when I went to my computer not knowing what I was going to write at all. I would fret and waste time and generally end up feeling like crap because my valuable writing time was ticking away and I had added no new words to the manuscript.

It didn't take me long before I realized I didn't want to have writing sessions like that. It sucked. Writing amazing fiction can be frustrating in a myriad of other ways, so I decided not to add to it by showing up at my computer without a plan.

The least frustrating way to write that I've found is to *always have a plan when you sit down.*

I started plotting the night before I wrote many years ago. I would not go to bed until I had at least one or two scenes figured out for the next day. This meant I had notes about what was going to happen in the scenes, who was going to do what, and often even dialogue lines. I did this for *years and years* every single night. When Jake became my primary plotting partner, he would get unbelievably high every night, and we would sit on the couch in our living room, where I would tell him what I wrote that day, and then, together, we would figure out what was coming next.

You could also call this "plotting as you go." Like I talked about earlier, I don't like to plot myself into a boring story that leaves no room for spontaneity or exciting surprises while writing. That also means I don't generally know what happens from scene to scene to get from point A to point B. That takes a village sometimes.

Talking it out with someone is an amazing way to help your creativity soar. And even better if they don't care that you reject a bunch of their ideas—kindly, of course. It takes a strong person to be my plotting partner. Sometimes, I reject *a lot* of ideas. They don't feel right. They don't fit with the things I know are coming later. But I'm so grateful for those ideas because I recognize that I don't always know what's right for the story at every given moment. Sometimes, I need to hear someone else throw out something as a springboard to get my mind back into the story and plotting with glee.

I'll never forget writing my second to last trilogy. I had *no idea* who the bad guy was going to be through the first two books. I mean, I thought I knew who it was going to be, but the story didn't go in that direction, and my vague idea for the villain didn't work. So, here I was, deadline looming, as always, 100,000 words already written, rolling into book three without any idea whodunit or how I was going to wrap up so many dangling plot lines in the final 60,000ish-word book of the trilogy.

To say I got myself into quite a pickle would be accurate. But I didn't panic. *Don't ever panic.* That helps *nothing.* There's always a solution. You just have to believe you can figure it out. We *always* figure it out.

So, instead of panicking, I took one of my favorite creativity tools—a giant easel pad—and wrote out all my loose ends in marker. I also made a list of every character and all their possible motives for being my "bad guy." I stuck them all on a giant picture window in our house, completely blocking our gorgeous view. Jake and I stared at those pages for quite some time.

Eventually, as it always does, a solution arose that fit perfectly. Actually, I had already subconsciously laid the groundwork for it in the story without even realizing what I'd done.

I often do that in books without realizing it. I throw out all sorts of things in stories as potential threads I can pick up and use later, or they end up being red herrings that throw readers off the scent of where I'm really going. Red herrings are something I learned about in law school from exams, which turned out to be extremely beneficial in writing suspenseful stories.

Thankfully, law school saved my butt with that trilogy, and it turned out phenomenally. It's truly one of my very favorite stories I've ever written. And that ending—it was a total shocker to the readers. Like I said, if I don't know what's coming, it's really hard for them to figure it out in advance.

Make sure you devote enough time to your story outside of the time you bank for your actual writing sessions. If you work a day job, I highly encourage, if possible, that you use your time on the job—sorry to your boss and company—to think about your book. I plotted and wrote my first nine books while practicing law about 60 hours per week. I devoted every free moment of mental space that I could between conference calls, drafting and negotiating contracts, and especially on my commute to my stories. I made use of every minute of my day that I possibly could. I wanted this dream to become a reality for me *very, very badly*, and I was willing to do whatever it took for me to get there.

If you have time that you would normally spend scrolling social media, shift to spending it plotting. Go to your keyboard and computer screen with more scenes than you have time to write. Do it again the next day. And the next day. And the next day. Eventually, you're going to have a finished manuscript that you can turn into something amazing.

Don't go to your keyboard with a blank screen in your mind. Have that movie you're translating into words ready to begin playing the moment you sit down and put your fingers on the keys.

That's my best advice for consistently producing great writing days, day after day, year after year, without feeling like you're working too hard, without major frustration, and without wanting to constantly slam your head in a door. Time is precious. Make the most of what you have and make it productive. Yes, it involves even more time, but it's worth it. Amazing fiction happens because you do all the necessary things to bring it to life. This is just one way to make it a little easier on yourself that I learned through trial and error over many years of experimenting with my own creative and production processes.

The Quality of Your Drafting

As a lawyer drafting and negotiating contracts nearly every day for eight years, I learned something really important. A contract can be drafted in a manner that leads to it being ugly, good, great, or elegant.

When you read an ugly contract, you know it. It gets the job done, but it's not pretty. It's like a ham-handed brute bludgeoned the concept you're trying to articulate into words. A good contract isn't ugly. A great contract is better than good. But an elegant contract, something I didn't even know could exist until I started working at a Fortune 50 company with lawyers who charged over a thousand dollars per hour, is on an altogether different level of creation and beauty. Complicated concepts are expressed simply, clearly, and beautifully. There's no question of the meaning of these complex situations because the contract was drafted with such thought, precision, and intentionally selected word choice that the exercise is taken to a totally different level. As odd as it sounds, it's truly a beautiful thing to witness, especially if all you've ever seen are ugly, good, and great contracts. I suppose you might have to draft and negotiate contracts almost daily for eight years to appreciate such a thing, but it taught me a valuable lesson that I carried over into my fiction.

As a reader and a writer, you're going to notice that books can be drafted in a manner that is ugly, good, great, or elegant. There are plenty of good stories that are written in a way that's just ugly. Sure, there are words on a page, but they're not pretty. They don't transport you to a different place or an alternate reality. You have to pick your way through the story to try to get to the point rather than allowing yourself to be consumed by the story.

With good drafting, you can get lost in the story. With great drafting, you can watch it more easily as a movie in your head. But occasionally, you find a story that is drafted so elegantly that you feel totally and completely inadequate as a writer and a storyteller. *Those* are the best stories to read to improve your drafting. Instead of allowing it to make you feel like you should never bother to write another book again for the rest of your life—and we've all felt that—you should take notes and learn from it.

Your drafting can always get better. There are always parts of the process where you get lazy. We can't help it. Writing books is a lot of work. Drafting amazing fiction elegantly … whoa, buddy. That's a lifelong goal you can work on daily.

The books that sell the most copies won't always be the best stories or the best written books. It's a fact. There are tons of factors that go into book sales, and often, the quality of the drafting isn't one of them. That's good for a lot of us though, I suppose. My work, because much of it was written on very short deadlines, doesn't approach the level of elegance that some other authors produce. However, not writing elegantly will not preclude you from writing amazing fiction. My personal experience and book sales back that up. In publishing, just like in life, we make trade-offs. Writing with great speed might mean you don't write with great elegance. Only you can decide what matters most to you during any given project.

All things created equally, I would suggest not writing so fast that the quality of your drafting suffers. If you're one of those souls that has a beautiful talent for writing elegantly, then do it.

And if that's more than you can handle thinking about right now, then don't worry about it. I didn't. Remember it later, when you've got the basics down and you're working on improving your writing. Because there's *always* something you can improve in your writing. You are never done getting better at this game. It is a lifelong learning experience.

However, you can choose to rest on your laurels and get by with good enough, but if you want to be remembered for writing truly amazing fiction, then elegant drafting could be exactly what you need to add to your recipe.

It can take more time. It takes a more selective choice of words. It takes tons of rewriting to make sure you're not using the same words over and over again—and you *will* have favorite words that you use *to death*, and they might change from book to book. Drafting with elegance might be something you naturally do—which is awesome! Some authors are just born writing like this. Others, like me, are not. All we can do is aspire to become better writers and hone our craft. It's like a perfect golf swing or the perfect line on a racetrack. Continuous improvement is the only path to perfection, and even then, it's not guaranteed. Lifetimes are spent honing skills like this. Don't get down on yourself if you're not the best at drafting straight out of the gate. That might take 20 books for you to get there. Who knows?

The most important part is that you're writing, and you'll keep getting better at it with each book. Give yourself time to become a master. They say that 10,000 hours of work in a particular discipline is the ticket to mastery. While I've spent over 10,000 hours reading, I haven't spent 10,000 hours with my hands on the keyboard, writing fiction, yet. My drafting continues to improve with each book, and so will yours. Just keep going.

Also, keep in mind, you are not manufacturing this story. It is art. It is a creation that you shape and perfect as it comes through you. Be the artist. Eventually, you'll become the master.

ELEVEN
PRICELESS PRO TIPS

Repeat after me: There's always a solution, and there's always a way to finish the book. Now that we're on the same page, let's dive into some of the best advice I can possibly give you.

Filling Your Plot Holes by Hand

This is going to sound too simple and too easy, but this is one of my most trusted, tried-and-true methods for figuring out what needs to happen next in a story: I close my computer, take out a pen and notebook, and write down my question.

What should she do next?

Then, I start stream-of-consciousness journaling. Whatever comes to mind first, I write it down. I write down an entire list of possibilities that could fit. Every single time— and I do mean, *every single time*—one possibility catches my imagination, and my stream-of-consciousness journaling takes on a life of its own. Which means, *Yay! Creative flow has gotten involved!*

All I do is keep writing down what comes into my mind, and the solution to what might have felt like a tricky plot problem appears, often with *a lot* more information about what comes next in the story that I wasn't even expecting.

Why does this work?

Freewriting in this way is extremely powerful. There's magic involved when you put pen to paper. And when you're totally focused and in solitude, you can use that pen and paper to connect with creative flow very easily.

When the solutions start coming through, it's almost as though I hear a voice in my head, and I'm just writing down everything it says. Sometimes, I have to pause, wait, listen, and reconnect to the flow with patience, but it's there. And when everything has come through that is needed, the flow stops, and I feel that I'm done receiving whatever was being offered to me by the genius of the Universe.

I cannot tell you how many times I've solved seemingly unsolvable plot problems with this very simple and easy method. I remember sitting on a bed at the Lake Austin Spa and Resort—where I've gone to start or finish many a project —staring at my blank notebook page, wondering how I was going to figure out how to land the plane on my third trilogy.

I had no idea what one of the cliff-hangers was going to be, and I had to make it awesome. There's nothing like putting boatloads of pressure on yourself to top every story, every time—something I don't recommend.

But that's what I was doing at the time.

I started writing down possibilities, and then, *bam*, I could *see it*. The scene came to life in my mind's eye. And, oh, it was awful. Painful. Horrible. My readers were going to hate me for that cliff-hanger. It was *perfect. Brilliant.* It worked amazingly well.

Without a pen and notepad, I never would have gotten to that solution.

Tapping into creative flow isn't hard. I wouldn't be surprised if most people make it way harder than it needs to be. Creative flow is quiet and efficient. It's pretty much always there when you need it, but you have to be in the right, receptive headspace and generally a pretty quiet environment so you can hear it and recognize it.

I am a creature of solitude. I love being alone. I love silence. That might make me weird, according to the judgment of others, but that's just how I'm built. Once I realized how quiet creative flow is, I realized why I loved silence so much—it's full of possibilities, and those are my favorite.

There are always answers for every single plot problem. There are always solutions. There is always a way to get your book back on track and finish it. It might not be the easiest solution. It might require a lot of work or for you to delete words and start going again in a different direction. But solutions are always available to you. Remember that. It makes it much easier to receive solutions when you believe they exist, and it's only a matter of time before they come to you. Conversely, if you believe that your plot problem is so tricky that it can never be solved, the book can't be fixed, and there's no way you can finish it … well, there's a good chance you might be right.

What you believe is often what you receive. Believe the

best about yourself and your work and then help that become your reality.

A few years ago, I undertook the biggest fiction project of my life. As of today, I'm still not sure how I'm going to pull it off. I try not to think too much about that though. It might make me worry or invite self-doubt. It's easier just to believe that the idea wouldn't have come to me and captured my attention solidly for four years if it wasn't meant to be born through me. Creative flow picked me for this story. Or maybe I picked it. I have no idea. But I do know that I wouldn't be working on it if it wasn't meant to come to life.

Your story came to you for a reason. That book is in your heart for a reason. Of course it can be written. Of course it can be finished. And, yes, it can be amazing.

As my mom always says, "What the mind can conceive and believe, man can achieve."

Believe in yourself. Believe in your story. Believe the Universe wants to help you bring it to life and will send you all the ideas, resources, people, inspiration, and tools necessary to make it so. Your job is to recognize and receive all the goodness being sent your way.

That song on the radio with the lyrics that totally get your mind spinning and running down a new direction for your story—a gift from the Universe.

That conversation you overhear while you're waiting in line that triggers a plot idea you totally wouldn't have had otherwise—a gift from the Universe.

That book you pick up that inspires you and solves the problem that you've been mulling over—a gift from the Universe.

And all you had to do was pay attention and be open to solutions. It's really magical when it all comes together. That's also why it's a process. It's not a one-and-done deal. It's constantly evolving work that's coming to life because it didn't exist before. And you're the one birthing it. Congratulations! That's freaking exciting!

And if you're wondering again, *Can I actually do this?* Yes. You can. You wouldn't want to do it so badly if you weren't meant to. Accept that achieving your goals and making your dreams reality aren't always easy, but if you're determined enough, it's always possible. Anything is possible —including finishing your book.

Avoiding the Dreaded Sagging Middle

I rarely struggle with a "sagging middle" in a book, but I hear other authors talk about this phenomenon often. I think Dwight V. Swain taught me so much about inching up the tension constantly during the story that the issue doesn't really enter into my world. But the first time I ran into a total blank wall and had no access to someone I trusted to brainstorm my way out of it and figure out how to make the book awesome, I came up with a rule of thumb that has served me well in such situations for more than 30 books.

If you don't know what to do in your story, blow something up or blow up someone's life, kill someone or kill their dreams.

I know it sounds horrible and terrible, and maybe it is. But it's a relatively surefire way to get your story moving again and keep your readers on the edge of their seats. I've done this more times than I can remember. No reader has ever noticed a pattern at this point either—although someone probably will now that I have spilled this secret that I've never shared before.

Why does this work? Change is interesting. It also gets your characters totally engaged with what is happening in their world. Facing unthinkable situations forces your character to respond and grow and transform into someone who can handle the crap you just threw at them. This little trick has brought out amazing scenes that are some of the most memorable that I've ever written.

You have to be able to throw crazy stuff at your characters. You might even feel mean. But it's not, ultimately. Life throws crazy stuff at each of us. It's not done out of cruelty though. It's so we can grow, evolve, and become stronger and wiser people than we were before. The hardest things I've been through in my life shaped and defined me. I wouldn't be who I am without having experienced those hard things. It's the same for your characters. We all get banged up with some bumps and bruises along the way on this wild ride called life, but our hearts heal and grow stronger each time.

Your characters can take it. You might find yourself reaching new depths in emotion with your writing as a result.

But please remember that there is a difference between throwing crazy stuff at your characters to help them transform and being cruel to them. Your readers can tell the difference. I've read some *depraved stuff* that authors did to their characters, and those scenes made me never purchase another book by those particular authors ever again. All readers have their own lines that they aren't cool with an author crossing, including me. There are a lot of things I don't want to read about, so I don't write about them.

Only you can decide what your lines are and what's okay with you to put in a book.

I've written some dark stuff, but I don't want to put dark, twisted, disturbing images into the subconscious minds of my readers or collective consciousness. These days, I think very carefully about what I put in writing in a book. I don't want to be the trigger that potentially brings a negative experience into the lives of my readers. We are responsible for our own creations. Just because other authors have no problem writing depravity, perversion, and some really, really, really dark and twisted stuff doesn't mean you have to in order to write amazing fiction. Every creative artist has their own lines and their own integrity. The most important thing is figuring out what yours are and writing stories that you'll be proud to publish and share with the world.

Plot Napping

I had no idea that I had stumbled upon one of the great secrets of creative genius when I began plot napping. I thought I was just being strategically lazy—something I'd always excelled at. What am I talking about? I don't know what it's really called, and Salvador Dali undoubtedly called it something else, but to me, it's a way to access magic.

Salvador Dali used to sit in his chair and nap briefly, holding a spoon in his hand, which would fall to the floor when he started to drift off—which meant he had reached the place where all answers existed, including to all creative quandaries.

Plot napping is something I've been doing for years, and it has solved countless of my creative quandaries. This is how it works: I need a piece of my plot, possibly the next scene that I need to write, and nothing is coming to me. Because I generally have a deadline of some sort, sometimes, I can't wait days or weeks for the answer to pop up. So, instead, I go directly to the Universe for help. How? I take my journal or notebook and a pen or pencil and cozy up in bed.

With my pen or pencil in hand, poised on the paper, I lie down and think about what I need to know. Sometimes, I'll write the major burning question I have down on the page.

For instance: *What would he do next?*

Then, I let myself drift off into dreamland—but I don't go all the way to sleep. I just … drift. I let go of all my thoughts, as if allowing my mind to go to sleep. It's almost like a meditative state, where I have no focus on anything, but I also don't care about trying not to think. I just … drift lightly toward a nap.

Somewhere in the ether, as I'm drifting off with that plot point question as the last thing on my mind, I can reach a place where all the answers and possible solutions exist. Whatever I need for my story is somewhere in collective consciousness—the Great One Mind.

When people say there's nothing new under the sun and that every story has already been written, I believe "they" are telling the truth. There is nothing new. Every story has been written. *But* it hasn't been written by you, filtered through the lens of your unique life experiences or with your twist, done in your style. That's your job.

But in the in-between, between wakefulness and sleep, there exists genius. It's a space on the threshold. A space where things are obvious. If you've never experienced it, it probably sounds batshit crazy. But I promise you, it is very real, this place that isn't a place, where creative geniuses go to find answers.

I stumbled upon this place that isn't a place purely by accident. I had no idea I was tapping into the very creative genius of the Universe when I discovered it.

And when I try to explain it to people, especially people who have no grasp of consciousness or how energy works, they think I'm batshit crazy too.

But this is a really useful tool regardless of how silly it sounds or how insane my explanation might appear to you.

Having access to the source of creative solutions is priceless. Knowing you can get there anytime you want by essentially just preparing to take a nap is *also priceless*.

I was once working on a trilogy when I shouldn't have been. I was incredibly stressed out, under major pressure, and totally burned out. But I wasn't smart enough back then to give myself the rest and recuperation I needed before diving into another major creative project. It was during this stressful mess of a project that plot napping became the only thing I could do to figure out the story and finish it.

I literally plot-napped every single day. I couldn't find all the answers to my story in my conscious working hours because I was simply a ball of stress in a bucket of self-doubt. But I'm also not a quitter, and I had a deadline to hit, so I sidestepped my stress and self-doubt and cut straight to solutions.

Every afternoon, I would lie, curled up in my bed, with my notebook and pen in hand, and I would write my question down on the page, release all my cares in the world, and drift off. In that limbo state, the next scene or fix to my plot would come right to me while half-asleep. I would scribble everything floating through my sleepy mind down on the page. I doubt I was fully conscious for most of it. I was simply desperate and willing to do anything I could to finish the story, top my previous trilogy, and hit my deadline— which I missed, by the way.

Creative flow saved me on that one. Hugely. I had known *nothing*. I'd had no idea where I was going with the story or how to make it work, and then, *bam*, I had enough of an answer that I could write another 6,000 or so words until I was once again clueless about what to write.

Long story short, all three books of that trilogy hit the *New York Times* Best Sellers list. Plot napping is for real. It's a tool used by many creative geniuses. I didn't invent it. I just discovered it by sleepy, happy accident and thought I was the only one who knew about it … until I started reading about Salvador Dali and others. Talk about a boost of creative confidence when you realize someone recognized by the world at large as a creative genius faithfully used the same tool you do when searching for creative solutions.

I'm almost positive that the brilliance of plot napping could be applied to many other issues needing solutions. However, I've only applied it to writing amazing fiction.

I can't wait to hear about how it changes your life and all

the other uses you might find for it. It is truly a simple gateway to magic.

The Days You Don't Want to Write

What do you do on the days you don't want to write? Especially those days when you have a deadline looming, but just can't seem to force yourself to sit down in front of your computer?

I can tell you what I used to do, and I can tell you what I do now.

First, what I used to do:

My prior editor required me to set deadlines with approximate word counts up to two years in advance. I don't know about you, but that didn't work very well for me. I had no idea what I was going to want to write in two years, let alone know how many books it would take or how many words they would be. That was pretty impossible for someone who writes with creative flow, like I do.

Other authors do fine with this system, however, because they operate more like a machine or an assembly line. For me, it created a nightmare that I lived in willingly for *years*.

Because of my ambitious publishing schedule, deadlines were always pressing. I had *two years of deadlines looming ahead of me* at any given moment. It was a lot of pressure because I had to deliver something that was at least close to what I'd said I would deliver years earlier or else go through the stress and pressure of trying to make changes to a date I'd agreed upon with my editor without impacting my publishing schedule. Again, it was a nightmare. But I did write a lot of books in a very short period of time because of this.

During this era of my life, when my deadlines generally provided me with around six weeks to write anywhere from one to three books, there were *always* days when I *did not want to write*. Like, at all. Some days, I would wake up, and I just couldn't do it. Writing sounded torturous. It was the last thing in the world I wanted to do even though I'd done it effortlessly the day before. Often, I literally couldn't force myself—not for all the love or money in the world—to even sit down in front of my keyboard and open up my manuscript. I just couldn't do it. Something in me was like, *Nope. Not today, sucker.*

It was always very painful because I was constantly aware of the days, hours, and minutes ticking down to my deadline.

So, what did I do?

I'll tell you what I didn't do—*write*. But I also didn't take the day off to enjoy myself either.

Nope, I didn't get any words down, and I also didn't take the much-needed day of rest and relaxation that my body, mind, and soul were obviously craving. Instead, I would take the day off from writing and spend all day beating myself up for not writing. I would feel like absolute and total crap. I would berate myself for not being able to push through and get more words down so I could stay on track. I would feel incredible guilt for not working on a day when I clearly wasn't meant to be working.

In a word, it *sucked*. It was miserable for me and everyone around me. I was no ray of sunshine, and my energy was *crap*.

At that time, I felt like if I let myself enjoy that day off, then somehow, I'd be transported to a universe where I might never have another productive day of writing at all. It was fear, guilt, stress, fatigue, and exhaustion, all blended up into a destructive cocktail that caused misery and suffering to everyone in my world that day.

Putting it in writing makes it sound a whole lot dumber than it felt at the time. Back then though, it felt like the world was ending because I couldn't get my words down and that my entire business might crumble because I was putting myself a day behind on my deadline. I gave myself no grace, no mercy, and I had no faith.

It wasn't a good or healthy way to live as a creative being. In fact, it just added to the suffocation I already felt under all those deadlines. It was awful and paralyzing. I don't recommend that route to anyone.

Instead, if you wake up one day, regardless of how close your deadline is, and you just *don't want to and can't make yourself write*, then it's an excellent moment to recognize how amazing your ability is to identify and meet your own needs.

"I don't want to write today," means that you want to do something else, or your body, mind, or soul *need* you to do something else. Take a breather. Take a break. Have some fun. Relax for a day. Give yourself grace. Recognize that creativity is not always an on-demand process. Sometimes, things that you think should keep going forward without a single pause for a breath of fresh air actually need more time to marinate and percolate.

And if you wake up two or three days in a row and you just *don't want to write and can't make yourself do it*, that's okay too. I've been there. You know what happened *every single time*—whether I beat myself up or let myself relax? An awesome, perfect, magical idea for the book came to me during that time when I was not writing. Something that made the entire story even better and added depth, richness, and magic that I never would've known was possible had I forced myself to keep going. Wild, right?

Eventually, after years of beating myself up, I started taking those days when I didn't want to write in stride. I'd affirmatively decide that I was taking the day off and I was not going to think about writing at all. I'd put my mind and effort into something else, or nothing at all, and just flow with the day. No guilt. No berating. No fear I'd miss my deadline. No anger. No pressure. No stress.

Talk about a game changer. And all I did was cut myself a break and I stopped being so dang hard on myself.

There's no need to flog yourself to creative death just because your body, mind, and soul need a break. I know how easy it is to fall into the trap of believing you can and should be able to do anything at every given moment regardless of how you feel. You might be a superhero, but even superheroes take days off to rest.

Forcing yourself to be constantly productive is a recipe for burnout.

Be careful with yourself. You matter. You create things that didn't exist before. You make magic. Don't treat yourself like a rented mule and beat yourself up constantly for not producing every word you think you should on every day you plan to write.

Be kind to yourself. Be fair to yourself. Have mercy on

yourself. I can't stress this enough. I didn't do these things soon enough, and they cost me more than I'll probably ever know. I have no idea how many more contemporary romance novels I would've written if I hadn't been so hard on myself and tried to force myself to do things that were ultimately inhumane.

Bottom line: Just because you can doesn't mean you should. While this applies across all areas of life and is something Jake and I both constantly say to each other, it especially applies to writing amazing fiction.

Just because you can force yourself to do something doesn't mean you should.

Just because you can write a book in a week doesn't mean you should.

Just because you can override your body and mind's natural need for rest and recharging doesn't mean you should.

Don't flame out before your time. Take care of yourself like you would the most precious of all the tools in your arsenal. Because you are. You are absolutely precious. The things you can do with your mind and your creativity are truly incredible. Recognize the value you bring to the world and treat yourself, your skills, your abilities, and your talents with reverence.

And above all, take a guilt-free day off when you need it. It does worlds of good and ultimately leads to the best story you could possibly write, and that's hugely important if you want to write amazing fiction.

It's Okay to Hate Your Book and Your Characters

It seems like there's always a point in the process where you hate your book or your characters. It's okay. I think that's pretty normal. You might think your book is the best thing ever created and the worst piece of garbage—all in the same day. Welcome to being an artist. There are a lot of ups and downs on this ride. Strap in and prepare for the roller coaster. You will doubt yourself and question yourself more than you probably ever have in your whole life. I'm pretty sure that's normal too.

Don't lose faith though if you hate your book. It is highly likely it's a passing moment of frustration or fatigue. Don't take those moments and make them your whole story. Give yourself some time, a break, a snack, a nap, some water, a walk in the woods, a swim, a workout, a bath, or something else to reset. Sometimes, it's best to save your draft, close the document, shut down your computer, and step away before you torch it with a flamethrower. Most likely you'll feel differently about your book when you come back to it, and whatever you were wrestling with will look different too.

I can't tell you how many times I've thought what I wrote is complete garbage. Just utter rubbish. No one can be harder on me than I am on myself. And then when I send it off to someone, expecting them to confirm my opinion of the garbage I wrote, I'm always pleasantly surprised to hear that what I wrote is actually pretty good. Maybe it needs fixing, or not, but it's usually way better than I thought it was.

As an artist and creator, you're too close to your work to

judge it objectively. You just can't do it. Your opinion of your work, while you're in the middle of it, might not be accurate at all.

The creative process and the process of creating amazing fiction is not an easy one. It will test you, make demands of you, push you, prod you, scare you, and make you wonder if you're absolutely insane. You might be. We all might be. Who knows?

But we do this because these stories cannot otherwise be enjoyed by our fellow humans if we do not take the time to translate the incredible, awesome, amazing ideas in our minds into readable, consumable, enjoyable books.

You're doing something magical. You're taking part in creative alchemy. That's a big thing. There is no one way to do this. No one can tell you how your process is supposed to go. That's something only you can figure out by doing it.

And, yes, there might be times when you hate your characters. There might be times when you want to chuck the whole freaking story and you wonder why you ever thought spending your time writing was a good idea. I promise you, I've experienced the entire gamut of emotions, feelings, and reactions while playing this creative game. And yet I cannot stop.

The ideas keep coming. The characters continue to be born. The stories keep forming. The plot twists keep popping up. It's an affliction, but one that I love and one I am clearly meant to be afflicted by.

You don't need to judge yourself or your process or your work in order for it to turn out beautifully and magically. You just need some faith in yourself and creative flow. It doesn't matter if you don't know what you're doing. It matters that you keep trying. It matters that you care enough about the idea in your mind to set aside the time and do the work necessary to bring it to life.

You might question everything when you're in the midst of your process, including why you're even alive. I've been there. Many of us have been there. Welcome to the team. We pluck magic out of the ether and turn it into memorable, amazing stories that the masses can experience. Does that sound easy? Does that sound quick? Or like something you can do without tons of thought, energy, and effort?

No. It's not.

But it's worth it.

Waking up every day and getting paid to write down the things you made up in your imagination is a pretty freaking fabulous way to live. The only limits are those you set yourself. And the upside? Well, J.K. Rowling was a billionaire before she gave millions away.

No one knows how your story is going to go, but writing that book in your head could change your life completely. It just takes one book for *everything* to change, but you never know which book it's going to be.

Go for it. And don't forget to give yourself grace. And if you want to pack all your characters into a car and blow the thing up with a car bomb so you don't have to finish writing the story, it's time to step away and give yourself a break. Come back when you're in a better headspace and ready to do the work.

Why I Don't Believe in Writer's Block

Yes, there are absolutely times when you do not want to—or cannot—write. It happens. Emotional devastation can easily do that to you. So can a lot of other things. But don't call it writer's block. Why would you cast that evil spell upon yourself?

You don't need an excuse not to write. Sometimes, you just don't want to write. As we talked about earlier, the creative process is not linear. This isn't a nine-to-five gig, where you just sit down and punch buttons or answer phones or do something you could do in your sleep. Creativity isn't like that at all. It's an interactive, living, constantly evolving force that is expressing itself through you. The state you are in when you sit down to write is really important. If you are stressed to the max and you feel like your life is burning down around you, *of course it's going to be harder to write amazing fiction.*

Jake and I were watching a documentary series on Fernando Alonso, one of the most decorated and talented race car drivers alive. One of the things I thought was really cool was how people in his life talked about creating an island of calm and peace around him. That's what it takes to perform at the highest level. Peace and calm. Not stress and fear. Peace and calm are expansive emotions. You feel more connected to life, which in turn means you're more connected to creative flow—to the infinite field of consciousness around us at all times. When you're stressed or in fear, you're restricting and contracting the flow of life through you. You're shutting out tons of amazingness because of your mental, emotional, psychological, physical, and spiritual states.

Then, there's that whole stereotype of the tortured artist, which I find to be extremely disturbing. Creating can be painful enough already because it is a birthing process—without any anesthesia. It's intense, dynamic, active, and demanding. Think about a woman giving birth naturally. She's a fierce creature in those moments, wild and raw, one with nature, doing exactly what her body was designed by Infinite Intelligence to do.

We were created to create. I firmly believe that's a huge part of why we are on this planet. To create. It's as natural as breathing for us. Creativity is a natural process. It's life, moving through you, expressing itself in ways that haven't been expressed through anyone else before. It's beautiful. It's magical. It's wild. It's unpredictable. And it's awe-inspiring.

But nature doesn't create every single day of the year. Even nature takes breaks. Winter comes, and life seems to die off or at least hibernate until the coming spring, when new life bursts through.

You are part of nature. You are not separate from her cycles or seasons. You are not meant to be productive every single day. Some days, you must rest. You must refill your creative well. You must be gentle with yourself and nurture yourself so that you can become all that you are destined to be.

So, yes. There will absolutely be days or seasons when you don't feel like writing. But it isn't "writer's block." That's just a dumb term that people use as an excuse. I think it makes some people feel important. Maybe it makes them feel more like a "real writer." But as a "real writer," I'm telling you that I don't buy that crap. I've never had writer's block. Ever.

What I have had are some really rough times in my life when I could barely function, let alone write.

The biggest reason behind why it took two years to finish my first book is that my dad was killed in a 15-car pileup about six months after I started it. Those aren't the kind of events you expect to happen to you, but sometimes, they do. It was devastating. My entire world imploded. I couldn't think, let alone write. I didn't care about anything and certainly not my book. I was just trying to survive what felt like an emotional and mental nuclear meltdown and find the strength to get out of bed the next morning.

That's not writer's block. That's life happening. It will always happen, whether you give it permission to or not.

Sure, there will always be people who say, "Channel those emotions into your books."

Well, Janet, when you're crying 23 hours per day, it's a little more complicated than it sounds. You might be able to turn around and channel emotional pain into your books as a way to work through it immediately. If so, bravo. I was not so evolved at that point in my life. It took me years before I could channel my grief into my work. It wasn't until a few years later that I poured a lot of that emotion into a story.

We all process emotion in our own way and at our own speed. Don't beat yourself up. Just recognize where you're at, and if it means you need to take some time for yourself and not focus on your work, then do that. Give yourself what you need. That's the most important thing. You don't have to be so strong that you just keep trucking through every single thing that happens without pausing to rest and recover. The better you can get at working and then pausing to rest and recover before beginning again, the more productive you'll ultimately end up being. Only channel those emotions into your work if it's genuinely healing for you. Don't feel like you have to.

Another time I totally could have blamed "writer's block" for not wanting to write was when I was attempting to write romance novels while going through a divorce. When you don't believe in love at all, even as a concept, there's a good chance it might be challenging to write romance novels.

I had taken six weeks off in between working for my old firm and going in-house for a Fortune 50 company, and I had planned to write and finish one book during my break.

Instead, semi-unexpectedly, I ended up filing for divorce. Talk about another emotionally devastating experience. I wasn't okay. I tried to force myself to write. Instead, I ended up plotting a story about a romance author who wrote the first two books of a trilogy and then didn't believe in love anymore, so she walked away, leaving this massively best-selling trilogy unfinished—to the horror of her readers—and became a motivational speaker, teaching people how to get rich.

I'm not joking. I really plotted that. Her readers tracked her down, and she ended up falling in love again and finished the trilogy for them.

Needless to say, I never wrote that story, but it was very telling about where I was in my life at that moment.

But I gave myself grace and just … tried to do what I could, when I could. It was really hard to let those beautiful six weeks of no day job slip by without finishing a book, but life doesn't usually go according to my plans. It usually has much better plans for me.

While I was freaking out about definitely missing my deadline, the Universe had a trick up its sleeve. By finishing the book months late, it turned out even better, and what's more, by releasing it months late, I was in perfect alignment with divine timing. That book became my breakout novel. It gave me a career. It hit *USA Today* three weeks in a row, about six weeks after my divorce was final. Not only that, but it sold 100,000 copies really quickly, and my first two books, which were flops, started selling amazingly well too.

With hindsight, I saw how much more complicated my life and my divorce could have become if I'd finished that book and released it before the judge signed off on the papers, protecting me from any financial claims regarding my books or my royalties.

Whether you recognize it or not while it's happening, life is always working in your best interest, even when it is totally jacking up your plans. I've had too many instances of things working out so much better than I could have ever imagined after I thought everything was going to pot.

Bottom line: If you don't want to write, there's a reason. It's not writer's block. It's you being human. It's fear, doubt, stress, negativity, emotional devastation, burnout, lack of self-belief, lack of self-respect, lack of boundaries, lack of time management, fatigue, overwhelm, hesitation, or something else. Your creativity will ebb and flow with your energy levels and your state of being. Learn how to meet your own needs the best you can, and you will do wonders for your productivity and your happiness.

Don't make excuses about why you don't want to write. Just quietly and without drama go about doing what you need to do for yourself. Take care of yourself. Give yourself what you need. There's a good chance you'll feel that creativity flowing again soon, and you'll be excited to write. And quite possibly, you could even be more productive than ever before after you've had some time to rest and recharge.

Become a Student of Your Craft and Fall in Love with the Process

The best way I know to continuously improve your creative work is to stay a student, keep learning, and fall in love with your process. Tweak, change, and optimize as you go, so it's easier and less painful to produce great work.

They say to follow your passion to your calling. Do what you love, and you'll never work a day in your life. I still feel like I'm working some days during my creative process, but most days, I'm having fun. The more you can enjoy the process, the more likely you'll have longevity and success as an author.

If you only love the finished book and the money it produces, you might struggle more. But be aware that you're not alone in that, and there's nothing wrong with you.

There was definitely a time in my life when the only parts of writing books that I enjoyed was the *ideation and plotting* part and then the *counting the money* part. Everything else in the middle had become a drag. I felt like I was living on a hamster wheel. I was writing too much, too fast, while not giving myself enough time to recover, let alone live a healthy, balanced life.

That led me to major burnout.

Falling in love with the process is key to avoiding burnout. If you love what you're doing every day, then how do you get burned out on it?

It's when you are constantly forcing yourself to do things you don't want to do that you become pretty miserable. I've done it. I don't recommend it.

Find a way to love your process. And if you don't love it every day, that's okay too. Loving it most days is plenty.

Never stop learning and never rest on your laurels. You will never know everything there is to know about writing fiction. I sure don't. I do, however, enjoy learning all the time. It doesn't have to be through reading craft books, although those can be *really helpful*. Read books you love. Read books that get you excited. Learn from other authors while they're showing you how amazing a reading experience can be.

There's one author I always go to, and I read three or four of her books before I start writing a new romance novel—Lisa Kleypas. For decades, she has been my unicorn author. To this day, I've never met her, but her books have had a massive influence on me, my writing, and my characters. She's one of the best in the business at doing what she does.

Figure out who your unicorn author is that inspires you and your work. Whose books can you read that will get you pumped up to try and create something just as magical?

Don't copy the person. Find inspiration in their work. Use that inspiration to make your work even better. That's what authors have been doing for ages, and it's just one more way to ensure your work reaches the level of amazing fiction.

Procrastination

Procrastination gets a bad rap, but it almost feels inevitable. There will always be those months, weeks, or days leading up to writing a book when I feel like I should be "doing more." I always wonder if I'm procrastinating or if I'm simply still in the preparation phase. I tend to go with how I feel and what I'm doing with my time to determine whether it's true procrastination. Am I making up every excuse I have not to start writing? Am I choosing to clean out and organize my closets and under-sink cabinets instead of starting the book? It might be procrastination. I also might just not be ready to start writing the book yet.

Sometimes, procrastination can be useful, but you ultimately need to recognize when it's time to just dive in and get down to writing. I feel an energy of urgency that comes upon me, or sometimes, an outside force will push me to start writing and help me to overcome the inertia. Eventually, I always start.

However, if you are procrastinating, know that all procrastination is not created equally. There is actually some super-useful stuff you can do while procrastinating that will help you become a better writer and author. If you don't feel like starting your book yet, for whatever reason, do some research, read writing craft books, study your genre or subgenre, read some more books you love, learn to use your writing tools, or just do nothing and rest. None of that stuff is wasted time regardless of it not adding word count to your book.

Don't be so hard on yourself. If there's a reason you don't want to write, honor it. However, there's always an exception to that rule. You must know yourself. It's the feeling you have while you're not writing that tells you whether you're avoiding it or whether you're simply not ready to start yet. Getting to know yourself, how you work, how your mind works, the games you play with yourself, the stories you tell yourself, and the excuses you make will ultimately help you become a much more productive writer.

I know when I don't want to write. I know when it's harmful to push myself to keep going. I know when I'm just not ready to start a book because there's something missing even if I don't know what that something is. You'll have to figure out all that stuff about yourself. Only you can do it. I can't tell you how to interpret your own inner guidance, but I can tell you it's there if you pay attention to it. And don't worry; at the end of the day, everything happens with perfect timing. If you're not ready yet, you're not ready yet. Don't beat yourself up. It won't help you in the long run.

Be kind to yourself. It's a lot better for your creativity and your soul.

Minimize Distractions

One of the most important decisions I've ever made in my life happened in 2014 when I decided to quit watching TV. I went at least six years without *ever* turning on a TV for *anything*. We don't have a TV in our house at all anymore. It might sound insane or hard-core to you, but for me, it was life-changing.

I knew if I wanted to be a successful author, I had to write books. Spending four-plus hours per day staring at a screen that wasn't my document was not helping me write books. In fact, the TV was making sure they didn't get written.

Sure, TV and movies can be great for ideas and give you tons of inspiration. That's awesome. I'm not saying I don't watch anything ever. I do. But at this stage of my life, I prefer consciously chosen entertainment for a limited duration.

For me, writing books takes a lot of time, energy, solitude, silence, and total focus. If I'm spending a big chunk of my day doing anything that doesn't create that environment, I'm not writing books during that time.

Scrolling social media became another giant distraction in my life after I quit TV. It took *years* for me to summon the strength and intention required to quit social media. I can't even begin to imagine how many hours of my life I wasted, scrolling through crap that didn't matter. Maybe as many as some people spend streaming their lives away.

At the end of the day, it doesn't matter what the distraction is. If it's keeping you from living your dream in reality, it's not helping you. Your attention and your energy are precious. *So precious.* Jake and I wrote about this in *A Creative Rebel's Guide to Winning the Game of Life*. The life you are living is a result of the decisions you've made, especially how you choose to spend your attention and energy.

When I quit watching TV and then quit spending any time at all on social media, my life changed. Dramatically. I became happier, more creative, more loving, and generally enjoyed life so much more and on so many different levels that weren't available to me while I was spending so much of my energy and attention being distracted.

When you focus your energy and attention on what you want, like becoming a successful author who writes amazing fiction, things *happen.* Things *change.* Because suddenly, you're a different person than you were when you were focusing your energy and attention on scrolling social media for hours per day or engaging in constant binge-watching marathons.

The number one thing unpublished authors say to me about why they haven't written or finished their book is this: *I don't have time.*

Ha. Does anyone have time?

You have time for what you value.

So, ask yourself, *What do I value?* Make a list.

Next, ask yourself, *What do I spend my time, energy, and attention on each day?* Make a list.

Now, compare your lists. How much time, energy, and attention do you spend on things that you value? How much time, energy, and attention do you spend on things that are meaningless and contribute nothing to your future? How much of your time, energy, and attention do you allow to be distracted away?

Change what you place your attention on and how you use your energy, and you will change your life. It's a universal law.

What about distractions that aren't screens, like people? What about your family and friends?

Yes, they count as distractions too. However, people are different than screens.

This is the time when you really have to determine what you want out of your life. If your goal in life includes writing an amazing book, you're going to need boundaries. Really super-awesome, incredible *boundaries.*

As I mentioned above, I took a three-year break from writing fiction. When I decided it was time for me to go back to writing fiction, it was *hard.* It took me *months* to reclaim my time, energy, and attention from all the different projects, people, and other random things that I'd spent it on without any restriction for years.

When I was writing fiction full-time, I didn't do that. I didn't have that much time, energy, or attention to go around. I could only do what I could do because I was using so much mental, emotional, creative, and physical energy to write my books. When I stopped writing fiction and stopped actively plotting at least three to six books at a time with an intent to write them as soon as possible, I freed up a lot of mental, emotional, creative, and physical energy that had to find new outlets. I'm an idea factory. I have to be working somehow. When I'm not burned out, I actually love to work.

Unplugging from all those outlets and taking my energy and attention back to focus on the one thing I wanted to create was one of the most painful things I'd ever had to do. Lord Almighty, it was shockingly hard.

There are people in almost everyone's life who require a lot of energy and attention. When creating amazing fiction and performing at a high level, those kinds of people have to be kept to a minimum in your life.

When I'm writing, very few people have access to me. *Very few*. During rewrites, sometimes, it's *only Jake*. I can't handle any more than that. It requires too much of my energy that I need to use to create something that has never existed in this dimension before. It takes a *massive* amount of energy to write amazing fiction. It takes a *ton* of your attention and focus.

I did it easily for years, and then I got out of my routines and habits because I was so burned out and couldn't continue. When I was finally healed again, I had to restructure my entire life, including my schedule, my routine, my businesses, and more, to be able to start writing again.

How you live your life will absolutely impact how you create. It can't *not*. They're one and the same.

The amount of distractions in your life and your boundaries, or lack thereof, will also heavily impact how much and how easily you create.

It matters. Everything matters.

So, what do you do if you have kids? *I have absolutely no idea*. I don't have kids. I don't have kids in my daily life at all. I live 30 hours away from my family. I don't have hordes of friends I keep up with. Actually, I only have a select few. I'm also not the person anyone calls when they need to be rescued.

My husband is my biggest distraction. He's also the love of my life and my soul mate. I spent the last three years hanging out with him as much as I possibly could. I adore being around him. But when it was time for me to start creating again, I had to make space and set boundaries with him too. Instead of spending most of our waking hours together, I had to start spending more time by myself. It was a hard change to make, especially because it's so easy to keep things the same as they are. It's especially hard when you're having so much fun together. I've had to overcome major inertia to get back into my creative zone, where the project I'm working on is important enough to me that I will make sacrifices to work on it.

When Jake and I first started dating, I told him, "I don't cook, clean, or do laundry."

I was 100% serious. I didn't do any of those things at the time. They weren't important to me. I spent that time writing books because I was working about 60 hours per week at my day job. I had to value every single spare minute I had in order for my dreams to come true.

You have to choose wisely how you spend your time, energy, and attention. You get what you pay for, especially with your attention. Would I be who I am today if I were still watching *NCIS* reruns? No, of course not. That Leroy Jethro Gibbs is too damn distracting.

TWELVE
ADVANCED STORYTELLING TECHNIQUES

Twists

A great twist, well executed, is a thing of beauty in fiction. Never underestimate the power of a great twist to take your book from okay to stunningly memorable.

I will never forget reading a novel by Alessandra Torre that had *the most epic twist* at the end. I was *stunned.* Shocked. In awe. Amazed. Immediately, I wrote down the editor of the book—and hired her later—and then I reread the book. How did she do it? How did she pull it off? I had to know.

It's through moments like those, as a reader, that I honed my skills for amazing fiction as an author. And one thing I love, almost above anything in fiction, is a great twist.

What is a twist exactly? It's when the reader thinks the story is going to go one way, and there's something shocking they don't know that will cause things to work out differently or be perceived differently by the reader.

As a reader, I got to the point where if a book didn't have a twist, I was kind of bored. I wanted to be wowed. I wanted to read memorable books that inspired awe because the author had pulled off something so magical. My taste as a reader has ultimately formed my fiction legacy as an author because all the things I personally love about fiction have filtered into my own work.

Long before Alessandra Torre, I was enamored of Sidney Sheldon. I'd started reading Sidney Sheldon books when I was 12. Definitely too young for a lot of them, but I turned out just fine, so I don't worry too much about that.

Sidney Sheldon had a few very specific elements that were in every book, and one of them was a shocking twist. Ahhhh … the memories I have of getting to that shocking moment when I finally learned the truth and I was just *flabbergasted. No. Way. She was the one who did it? Because why? Holy crap.*

I loved to ride that emotional roller coaster as a reader, which then made me into the author I became. I wanted to deliver those same shocking, spellbinding, awe-inspiring moments to my readers.

So, I learned how to do it, and I did it.

Talk about reader loyalty.

When someone can only get that kind of fix from you, they will keep coming back for more over and over again. Jake and I often joke about some of my books as being literary crack. Readers are obsessed with them. And as a literary crack dealer, I always have a market for my work because it's well loved.

People love surprises, even when they say they don't.

Surprises keep life interesting. And as I've stated more than once, life is too short to read boring books. Keep them interesting. Twists are a *great* way to do that.

How do you write a twist? I can't say I know a great formula for coming up with one, but if you intend that the story you are writing is going to have a great twist in it somewhere, then you need to start thinking about it. Thinking about it puts creative flow on notice that you need a good idea for a great twist. It might sound silly and simplistic, but I do believe that just deciding you need an awesome twist for your story is a huge part of making it happen.

A twist is ultimately something you, as the author, know that the reader doesn't know. You save that knowledge until the perfect moment, the perfect scene, the perfect timing, and then you deploy it for maximum emotional impact and shock value. As you likely already know, timing is *everything*.

Many of my conversations with my developmental editors over the years have centered around emotional impact. I'm always after maximum impact. Maximum emotional impact leads to memorable fiction. If someone remembers your story, it was hopefully a good one.

If readers forget basically every detail after they close your book, your work probably didn't have an emotional impact on them.

You are the conductor of your readers' emotions throughout the story. You might not know exactly how they're going to react, but you decide how to play it and how to write it to get the most impact out of your shocking twist.

One of my developmental editors didn't think it was important to keep things from readers. She would say things along the lines of, "If the reader knows, it's not a big deal. It'll still be a good book."

But good books have never really been my goal. I want to write and read amazing books. Amazing books, from my very personal view, require emotional impact, which often means that I keep secrets from my readers. Sometimes, I keep *huge secrets* from my readers.

I only do that because I want to give them the best reading experience I possibly can. As a hard-core reader, that's what I appreciate, so as an author, that's what I try to deliver every single time.

However, you don't always have to plot out a twist in advance and know exactly which things you're deliberately keeping from readers. Sometimes, the very best twists are ones that you, as the author, have no idea are coming. How is that possible?

Sometimes, characters keep secrets from *you*.

The first time I ever had this happen was a moment I will never forget. I believe it was a massive turning point in my literary career. I was working on my second book when I was *completely shocked* by what a character had kept from me. The story was about a girl who was keeping her identity hidden because she was largely hated by the world for something her father had done, and I thought *no one* in my story knew who she really was.

It turned out, I was wrong.

A side character, who I absolutely adored, somehow *knew* the heroine's secret. Not only that, but he also revealed that fact at a key moment in the book. As soon as the words flew from my mind through my fingers and onto the page, my jaw dropped. I was *totally stunned.* I'd had no idea I was about to type that. I'd had no idea that twist was coming.

"What? You *knew*! You knew, and *you didn't tell me*? How?" That was me yelling in my living room, staring at my laptop, dumbfounded by my character.

He had known something I hadn't known he knew. And he revealed it at a moment I'd least expected. I was *astounded.* It was *awesome.* It was one of those life-changing moments when I realized that it wasn't just me writing the story. There was way more happening than I understood. I hadn't known my characters could keep secrets from me. I hadn't known that I could write something without knowing it was coming.

It turns out, however, they can, and you can. *That* is the magic of creative flow coming to life right in front of your face. And, wow, it's *amazing.*

It was a twist that I hadn't seen coming on so many levels.

Were readers as shocked by the twist as I was? Who knows? But I can tell you the absolute truth—I'd had no idea, and it was the coolest experience I'd ever had while writing up to that point. I think that's the moment when I was really, truly hooked on writing fiction.

A good twist can be deployed in many different ways. My best advice is to read a lot of books in search of authors who do it well. Emulate their style, but don't copy it exactly. You're better than that and more creative. Eventually, you'll develop your own style for a twist, and others will emulate how you do it. It's a beautiful and never-ending cycle of creation and inspiration.

Red Herrings

I mentioned red herrings briefly before, but they deserve more discussion. Red herrings are *fabulous* devices for throwing off your readers when you're trying to be tricky or twisty. What is a red herring? It's a fish. What is it in writing? It's a tool of misdirection. It's something meant to confuse you and take you down the wrong road.

As previously stated, red herrings became part of my life in law school. Law school finals are a trip. You generally have the entire semester's grade riding on one exam. You don't have midterms or any other projects that count toward the grade for your class. It's literally *just the final*. Talk about stressful, right?

Law school finals are also a trip because they are long, involved, and complicated. They're always trying to mess you up. The "problem" is called a "fact pattern," and it's basically a story that the professor has written with all sorts of facts and conflict and things happening. Your job, as a budding young lawyer, is to read this fact pattern with the correct way of thinking and be able to identify all the important points while ignoring the red herrings that would send your analysis down the completely wrong road and trash your grade for the semester.

Law students have a great reason to be able to identify red herrings. It's usually something that seems too obvious to be the right answer. Or it can be a great red herring, which seems like it is *definitely* the right answer, but maybe for the wrong reasons.

I incorporated red herrings into my fiction because I didn't want readers to be able to figure out my twists in advance. I wanted them to think one thing and then feel that epic moment of shock and surprise when they realized they hadn't actually known what was coming.

I *love* that moment of shock and surprise. I write that moment with all due care. I also lay the groundwork for it early and often. If you want readers to be surprised by an epic twist, you have to give them something else to think about along the way. If you don't camouflage any of the twist, it might not be a very shocking and memorable one. It's okay. My first attempt at a twist was done like a total amateur, and I'm pretty sure it was totally obvious and not surprising at all. It wasn't exactly the most shocking and emotionally impactful moment I've ever written. But that's okay. We all start somewhere. Then, we resolve to get better at it the next time.

When I'm writing my first draft, I toss out all sorts of breadcrumbs and potential red herrings. At the time, I generally have no idea what I'm going to use them for down the road. I just know I need threads out there to grasp on to later when I'm weaving this whole masterpiece together. A little comment here, an object sitting on a table there, a chance meeting, a strange occurrence, a "random" encounter, et cetera. It doesn't really matter what it is. I do this completely by intuition and instinct. I don't have any rule of thumb on how to do this. I just do it naturally.

Leave yourself some interesting threads as you write. You don't necessarily have to tie them all up into a neat little bow to make the book awesome. Sometimes, it's just a throwaway line. Or when you're three books deep into your trilogy, you might remember and thank God that you added some little tidbit or random character in book one that can now come back and help you fix your plot issue and tie up the entire story into a fabulous conclusion that makes you look like an absolute creative genius … when you totally didn't plan it.

Leave yourself options. Throw out threads you can pick up later, when you realize you need them. Try not to write yourself into corners. Keep your twists concealed so you can unleash the truth on the reader in a way that creates maximum emotional impact. Red herrings can help you by throwing readers off your scent and allow you to do some creative acrobatics that will result in amazing fiction.

Flashbacks

Flashbacks are a tricky one. You have to pull them off well, or they don't really work. As a general rule of thumb, use flashbacks sparingly. Only use them to make a solid impact. Don't just flash back to something in the past because you don't know what's happening in the present—although I'm sure I've done that before too.

Flashbacks can be really jarring to readers, so make sure it serves the story well and that it is placed in the right spot for maximum impact. What is the right spot? I don't know. Only you and your story can answer that question.

I've used a flashback as the first scene in the second and third book of many of my trilogies. Why? The first time, it just felt absolutely right. I needed readers to fall in love with my thoroughly unlikable—and absolutely ruthless—anti-hero. I was already in love with his character because I knew what he'd been through to become who he became. The author *always* knows way more than the readers know about characters. I knew that by starting the second book with a flashback to his origin story, readers would see him in a completely different light. I needed to show them that anti-heroes weren't just born this way; they were made.

It worked so well that I kept doing it. Readers were practically begging for relief after my wicked cliff-hangers, but it didn't feel right to jump back immediately into the present-day scene in the first chapter of the next book. Flashing back to the past seemed to set the stage perfectly for the rest of the present-day story that followed. I've used flashbacks in a lot more books than just those though, especially when the characters have history together that's more fun to show the reader than to tell about it.

Use a flashback when it feels like the story is better for having it there. It must add some kind of emotional impact or relevant or fascinating character backstory or something else that the reader really wants to know or needs to know in order to understand the story better.

I personally avoided flashbacks in many of my earlier books because I think they're easy to do poorly. Learn how to use them effectively, and they'll add richness, suspense, drama, and impact to your fiction.

Bottom line: If you can't use a flashback correctly, you're better off not using them at all. Wait until they really make sense to use and feel right. Not every single book needs a flashback. Feel the story and go with what makes sense to you in the moment. Remember, you're the god of this world you're creating. Every decision lies with you. If you aren't comfortable using a particular storytelling technique or device, you don't have to. Eventually, you'll find a place where it works perfectly, even surprising yourself with how capable of a writer you have become.

Cliff-Hangers

My stance on cliff-hangers can be summed up as follows: *make them memorable*. I don't care what you have to do, but make the freaking thing memorable. Use shocking events. Drop twists *no one* sees coming. Unleash massive emotional pain if you have to. I don't care what it takes—you have to make the cliff-hanger *hurt*. You have to make the reader so desperate to know what happens next that they will wait with bated breath to buy the next book and the next book—with an equally incredible story inside, obviously.

Cliff-hangers are an art. You have to fulfill what I stated above, but you should also do it with style. With sleight of hand. With an epic last moment. Don't bludgeon the reader to death with it. Don't kill their hopes. Don't destroy their dreams. Don't be cruel. Reader trust is a fragile thing. You can't take that trust lightly, and I highly suggest you value it greatly for the best outcomes. A reader needs to know they are safe with you. They need to know you will take them through an epic adventure, which might be painful at times, but will ultimately satisfy them and fulfill the promise you made to them at the outset. If you have that, then readers will follow you pretty much anywhere. But know that there are lines. Some authors cross them repeatedly. And some even get away with it.

I can be "mean" to my characters. I can be *gut-wrenching*

to my readers. But I have lines that I will not cross. Not for anything in the world. Perhaps it's a consequence of reading so much commercial fiction, especially romance, for decades. But there are lines I don't think are acceptable to be crossed in books. And what's even more, Jake has his own set-in-stone lines that he will not cross.

Jake is my partner in everything I write. I tell him what I'm thinking about, which direction I plan to go, and I give him chunks of plot to chew on and ask for his advice and ideas constantly. There have been plenty of times where he has stopped me on something I wanted to write with a big fat no. He has often been the one to tell me that I can't go there. He has hard noes that are hardwired into his DNA by virtue of being a real, honest-to-God alpha male who answers only to himself and the Almighty.

There are boundaries in fiction I have been willing to push—something I learned along the way by doing—driven by our collective integrity, whether or not that's readily apparent. But people change, and so do their books. Your essence shines through your creations. You can't stop it. It's impossible. It's born through you. Through the lens of your experience. Through your consciousness. What you create will indelibly have your stamp upon it so sharply that those who know you well will be able to see you in it. And you, yourself, with honesty and hindsight, will see yourself in your creations as well. It's impossible not to. We are our art.

If you want to write great cliff-hangers, care about the reader's experience. Know what you love as a reader and then write that.

I was gobsmacked by a cliff-hanger by Aleatha Romig

once upon a time, and it changed my life. I was *speechless*. Stunned. Absolutely shocked. It was masterful. I adored it, even as I was sitting on my couch with my mouth hanging open, desperate to know what was going to happen next.

But I was also in awe. *How did she do that?* Immediately, I knew I wanted to be able to write like that too. I wanted to be able to deliver that kind of experience to a reader. It was epic. It was beyond memorable. The feeling it gave me was incredible and absolutely unforgettable.

So, I taught myself how to do it. I am my own first reader. I love books. I love to read. I love to get lost in a story that captures my attention and keeps it until the very end. I love good storytelling. Great character development. Incredible heroes. Strong heroines. Memorable and colorful side characters. Conflict that totally makes sense within the world the author has created. I want to suspend reality completely and immerse myself in the creation of another. It's like stepping inside someone else's mind. I'm so grateful that they wrote it so I could experience it.

Those are the stories I try to create every time. Something I like to read. And I'm a tough critic. I've read so many books. I know what I like. That's what I try to create for myself to read every time.

My highest praise for my own books is this: "If someone else had written this book, I'd think it was really, really, really good." I can picture Jake shaking his head at me as I say it too.

I love a great scene, but what's more, I *adore* a great cliff-hanger.

This is why I write them with such care. I care deeply

about the experience the reader has while reading the cliff-hanger.

It has to be memorable. In order to make it memorable, sometimes, it has to hurt, just a little. Sometimes more. A little bit of pain mixed with the shocking moment of your cliff-hanger makes for that *burned into your memory* experience. It needs to create a moment of intense emotional impact on the reader that he or she will never forget.

If a reader doesn't remember the end of your book and it was a cliff-hanger … they probably aren't going to buy the next one. I know because I've tapped out on a lot of trilogies in my life. I've always been my own target market and most of my own market research.

I am the reason I write books the way I write them. I write what I love. And I love an epic, unforgettable cliff-hanger.

If you're going to write cliff-hangers, *make them memorable.* Make them *amazing.* Make them shocking. Make them emotional. Make them a little painful. You'll sell more books. It's pretty much that simple.

The Truth about Trilogies—The Good, the Bad, and the Ugly

When I started writing my first trilogy, everyone said they were sick of trilogies after the flood that followed the Fifty Shades phenomenon. On top of that, readers were also supposedly sick of billionaires. Guess what my first trilogy was called? Dirty Billionaire. Yep, so you could say that I was willing to take a gamble on what my gut was telling me to do when everyone else was telling me I was crazy.

Thankfully, it was the right choice, and that trilogy grossed well over a million dollars.

I did not set out to write trilogies only. I just discovered I had a knack for it because I enjoyed writing twists and cliffhangers so much. Eventually, my readers nicknamed me the Queen of Cliff-Hangers, and successful authors were asking me for my trilogy writing tips.

But you don't have to ask. I'm just going to tell you everything I told them—and more.

Everyone always wants to know how to write a trilogy or how to decide that you need to write a trilogy. Here's my answer: Does your story merit more than one book? That's a legitimate question you have to ask yourself before you even consider writing a trilogy.

How can you tell if it does? Ask yourself these questions about your story idea: Is it a complex story idea with layered characters that are flawed and can have significant growth? Does it have adequate amounts of external conflict? Does it have subplots galore? Can you, as the author, stomach the thought of writing about these particular characters, their lives, and their conflicts for 150,000 to a quarter million or more words?

If the answer to any of these questions is no, then a trilogy is likely not a good choice. The worst thing you can do is write one book, chop it into three parts at semi-suspenseful points, and then call it a trilogy. To this day, I'm pretty sure there are still people who think that's what I do. It's not. Writing a trilogy that qualifies as amazing fiction is a lot more complicated than that.

Let's dive into the good, the bad, and the ugly, and then you can decide if trilogies are right for you.

The good: Writing a trilogy allows you, as the creator, to take a deep dive into your characters, plot, and subplots. You can have complex stories play out over more pages and more books, which gives you the ability to write twisty, shocking things that are really fun to write and read. Also, if you're self-published, it presents a great opportunity for marketing down the road. You can always discount the first book or offer it to readers for free as a risk-free trial of your work in hopes that they will purchase the next two books. If the story is written well and the cliff-hanger is executed fabulously, you can turn the trilogy into literary crack for readers. A trilogy beloved by readers is a massive asset in your backlist.

The bad: Writing a trilogy is a test of endurance. You're writing anywhere from 150,000 to a quarter of a million or more words about the same characters, possibly in one go. This is the way I preferred to write trilogies—all at once. I wouldn't release the first book until the third book was totally drafted. I learned this tip from Alessandra Torre many years ago. She released the first book in a trilogy that went to the moon and created a huge audience for her. However, according to her, readers were *relentless* about hounding her for the second book. The stress of such a situation like that does not sound enjoyable to me, nor did it sound like it was enjoyable for her. This level of pressure can make it harder to create and harder to relax into creative flow and do your best work. Also, if you don't write all three books at the same time, then you might be precluding yourself from making the trilogy *absolutely mind-*

blowing. If you write and release book one and then later have an idea for book three that would make the trilogy absolutely *amazing* and *unforgettable* but it requires a change in book one to make it work ... well, you can't. This can result in you potentially writing yourself into a corner that is tricky to get out of in a way that still produces amazing fiction. Excellent trilogies, in my experience, come about as nonlinear and holistic creative works, and if you leave the door open to be able to make small changes in earlier books, you can blow the minds of your readers and turn yourself into a major must-read author. But it requires sustained effort, determination, patience, and *a lot* of work. It's a marathon, not a sprint.

The ugly: Readers aren't always thrilled that you're writing a cliff-hanger. There are cliff-hanger haters out there who will never buy your books *ever* because they *absolutely cannot stand cliff-hangers.* Many of these readers have been burned multiple times by authors not living up to their promises when it comes to releasing a story that spans multiple books containing cliff-hangers. This is another reason I have always chosen to write the entire trilogy first and be very open and transparent with my readers to set their expectations accordingly. With all three books finished, I can set release dates in stone and always deliver what I promised to my readers. I am 1,000% in favor of telling readers in advance, or in the synopsis, that the story is a trilogy. I have seen it go so badly for authors who sneak a cliff-hanger into a book that their readers believed was a stand-alone novel. Sometimes, the backlash is significant, and you can read all about it in their angry reviews. However, I have also seen authors get away with this, and their readers don't care nearly as much as others. It truly depends on the author, their readers, and the relationship they have with them. I choose honesty and transparency because that's how I like to be treated as a reader. I don't enjoy jumping into a story, thinking I'm going to get my satisfaction and a conclusion in one book, only to find out at the end that I have to wait another year for a second installment. Some people are fine with that surprise. Others aren't. Only you can decide how to handle your business if you take the trilogy road.

The big upside: When all three books of a trilogy have been released, readers tend to love the depth of the story and the long-term character development and transformation. Trilogies are more than books. They're experiences. That is, if they're done well. Readers fall in love with these characters at a much deeper level because they've gone through so much with them. It's truly a magical experience.

Another big upside: Trilogies can be very profitable, but *only* if you really nail book one. The biggest concern authors generally have about writing trilogies is book two. And, yes, it *absolutely* needs to be *better* than book one. This is why not all stories can be trilogies. Not all stories can handle the rigorous demands of a trilogy to offer up an incredible reader experience for three books straight. You have to be able to pick up the pace of the action—and the relationship, if it's a romance—in book two. To me, the sign of a successful trilogy is how much people love book two. For most of my trilogies, book two is often a reader's favorite.

If you want to know if you nailed a trilogy, all you have to do is look at the read-through rate after it has been fully released for a while. Do the calculations to figure out what percentage of people are reading through from book one to book three. That will give you your answer as to whether you really did your job as an author—to keep people hooked on the story until the very last page. Several of my trilogies have read-through rates between 85% and 95%.

When I said that I considered it my job as an author to hook readers on the very first page and not let them go until the very last one, I wasn't kidding. That's how I've always written my books, and it has always paid off—especially in trilogies.

THIRTEEN
WRITING ROMANCE

Every story has romance, it seems—at least, most of the good ones. There's a romance slipped into just about every movie plot line.

Die Hard has romance.

Transformers has romance.

Black Panther has romance.

Star Wars has romance.

I could keep going all day. People love happily ever afters and love triumphing over all. It's hardwired into our DNA. People love *love*.

While I can't teach you everything I know about writing romance in one chapter, I can share with you some of the most important pieces of the puzzle if you're going to add romance to your story.

Admire and Desire

One of my developmental editors swore by this combination for writing amazing romance. She had learned these two important characteristics from her grandparents and their relationship: admiration and desire. It's not enough to have simply one of them for a great romance. Admiration alone can be platonic love. Desire alone is simply lust, not love. But when you combine admiration and desire, you have the building blocks of a great love story. Romance is the frosting on the cake. It's the beautiful and sweet part that most everyone loves.

Your hero and your heroine should both exhibit admiration and desire for the other. If they don't genuinely admire and desire each other within the pages of your story, then the reader isn't going to experience an epic romance. The reader might not know what exactly is missing, but something will feel like it is.

If you are in a place in your personal life where you're not a big believer in love and you don't particularly admire or desire anything about the sex of the person you're writing about, then you might struggle with this. It's okay. I've been there too. It's extremely hard to write romance when you don't believe in love.

As I mentioned previously, I was in the middle of writing my breakout novel while I was going through a divorce. I couldn't write for weeks. I didn't believe in love at all anymore, it seemed, which made it nearly impossible to write about love conquering all. From personal experience, I can tell you that if I had pushed myself to write the book anyway and finished it while in that mindset, it would not have been my breakout novel.

I stepped back from it and started writing something else instead. A novel about a total asshole of a man who I didn't particularly like at first. But the character had stormed into my head while I was plastered on Coco Loco in the Dominican Republic, getting drunk on a beach for eight days after I filed for divorce, and demanded to be heard. I gave him a voice, but I couldn't get back to my soon-to-be breakout novel and make serious progress on it for months. If you find yourself not liking your hero or heroine and you are writing a romance novel, you need to come back to focusing on admire and desire—unless you're writing an asshole character and you don't care if your readers might not like him.

Bottom line: Your characters must find something in each other to admire and desire, which means *you* must fall in love with each of them. The more you love the hero and the heroine, the more epic their romance will become. Beauty is in the eye of the beholder. If you see your characters' unique beauty and write it in a way that enables the reader to be able to experience it too, it's not too hard to help readers fall in love with your characters—especially while the characters are falling in love with each other.

A great romance is like a tennis match. The ball goes back and forth from the hero's court to the heroine's. Have fun with it. Admiration and desire make it authentic and exciting to fall in love through the pages of your story, and they help build a realistic and solid relationship between the characters, based on mutual respect, admiration, and desire. People love *love*, so give them what they want.

Strong Heroes and Heroines

All the heroes I've written since 2015 have been largely based on my now husband. He's a true red-blooded alpha male. He's the kind of man I used to read about in many ultra-addictive Kristen Ashley romance novels. When I had the chance to meet her in person for the first time, I asked Kristen Ashley if these kinds of men she wrote about were real, and she told me that every single man in her life—with the exception of her ex-husband—was an alpha male. I was stunned and floored. *This rare species of man is actually real? Whoa.* That was a life-changing realization. That was June 2015. Little did I know that, in a few short weeks, I'd be swept up in the most epic, book-worthy romance of my own with a man who was very much like those I'd read about in romance novels. They do exist. They are real. *And they're amazing.* Perhaps an alpha male is not for everyone, but mine is definitely for me.

When you're creating heroes and heroines, the most important piece of the puzzle is that *you* love the characters. *You* have to fall in love with them first, before your readers can. If you don't love your hero and heroine when you're writing romance, it's a lot tougher to write and sell a love story between them to your readers. You have to believe it first. You have to fall in love with their love first.

So, how do you create heroes and heroines who inspire that kind of love? I believe it's something you have to figure out for yourself. You are unique. The kind of heroes and heroines that appeal to you this strongly will be dictated by your own unique personality and experiences in life. What you love might not be what I love, which is totally fine and absolutely perfect. There are billions of readers out there, and they don't all want the same things out of their books, their heroes, or their heroines. Write about heroes and heroines who inspire your love and devotion, and your readers will undoubtedly find something to love and be devoted to as well.

However, there's another important point to mention that took me many years to learn and understand, which can help immensely in crafting strong heroes and heroines. There are two types of energy that exist within each of us—masculine energy and feminine energy. It doesn't matter if you're male or female. You have both. Either type of energy can be healed or wounded. A strong, incredible hero has beautiful healed masculine and feminine energy within him, as does a strong, incredible heroine.

The feminine energy might present in knowing when to pause, wait, and surrender. It helps us learn to go with the flow and surf the ever-evolving currents of life on the way to our divine destiny without drowning among the waves. It is about learning to be moved instead of always being the one doing the moving. We see it when we follow our instincts and intuition. It's following our gut and listening to the wisdom of our bodies and those things that we know without knowing how we know them. Jake has taught me so much about what it is like to live with and love a man who is supremely masculine but also has healed feminine energy inside of him. It's absolutely divine to witness and experience, and there's no question of how it leads to lifelong admiration, desire, love, and devotion.

On the flip side is healed masculine energy. It presents itself in knowing when to take charge, take action, and take initiative. It includes confidence and belief in ourselves that help us to know that we are enough, that we are worthy, that our ideas, work, and creations are worthwhile, and even more so, that they are worth the time, energy, effort, and discipline it takes to bring them to life. Healed masculine energy is beautiful to witness in a female or a male. It's a zest for life and the daring to go out and live it to the fullest.

When a person, real or fictional, has both healed masculine and healed feminine energy within them, you know it. You can't miss it. They're truly a horse of a different color. They live life on a different wavelength because they're healed instead of wounded.

Without both healed masculine energy and healed feminine energy, characters can become something else. A strong heroine can be perceived as a bitch if she doesn't have both healed masculine and feminine energy within her. A strong hero can be perceived as a dominating tyrant and asshole if he doesn't have both healed masculine and feminine energy within him.

It's okay if your hero or heroine starts off as unhealed during your story. That's totally fine—actually, it's *ideal*. That means you have something to work with to transform the character. The conflict and events of the story should lead to the character's healing and wholeness on an internal as well as external level. It's the growth and transformation of the character that matters the most to the story. Readers can hate the character in the beginning but love him or her in the end. That's a huge victory actually. I have had readers hate a hero through the entire first book of a trilogy, only to become his biggest, most devoted, and obsessed fans by the end of the story.

By healing the wounds of your characters throughout the story, you're setting them up to live an epic and believable happily ever after. The characters have to change to get there. For best results in romance, they have to change and grow *together*. They each have to learn their lessons. They each have to realize what's truly important so they can be vulnerable and open to life and love and become the person they're meant to be.

It's a balance of healed masculine energy and healed feminine energy that gives the impression of not only strength, confidence, and courage, but also kindness, mercy, and gentleness. It takes incredible strength to be merciful and gentle, whether we're talking in real life or in fiction. Weak people and weak characters are not capable of that because it is beyond their capacity. But like weak people, weak characters can become strong through facing challenges that require them to dig deeper and evolve to rise to the occasion.

Also, a character with both healed masculine and feminine energy lives more from the heart, making decisions in a different way than a character led by ego or living from fear. There's a big difference in effect even if it's hard to recognize at first.

To write strong heroes and heroines, some level of both healed masculine and feminine energy is necessary. I'm absolutely not saying your characters need to be perfect because perfect characters are boring and unrealistic, but some level of inner faith, confidence, and kindness from your characters is generally necessary for a great love story.

Don't write helpless heroines and weak heroes. That's no service to your readers, your characters, or the future you're helping to create with your art.

If you aren't strong, brave, or courageous or if you have little self-confidence or self-belief, don't worry. By writing stronger characters who have the guts and courage to say the things you wish you were brave enough to say and do the things you wish you had the guts to do, *you will personally grow stronger and more courageous.* Writing strong heroes and heroines will change you as a person. I swear it's true. It happened to me. You are living as your characters as you write your story. You are seeing the world through their eyes, with their bravery and strength. It changes you. You filter into your characters, and your characters become part of you. It might be totally subconscious, but it happens. You can't avoid it. You cannot write a character well and be completely unchanged by the experience. Remember that. Create your characters wisely. Make sure you want to live as them because for the length of time it takes you to write an amazing fiction story, you will live, eat, breathe, sleep, and dream of them—if you're lucky.

Make sure your characters are people you want to spend a lot of time with. If you love your characters and love to spend time with them, readers probably will too. Those are the characters who will become like old friends. Readers will go back to those books and reread them over and over again because they love them and wish those characters were their best friends or their loves in real life.

After all, that's what readers seem to be after—that which they cannot find in real life. Give them what they lack.

Hopefully, you're also helping to create stronger men and women in our reality, leading to a better outcome on Earth for us all.

Modeling Healthy Relationships

I've written a lot of romance novels in my day, but I've read even more of them. *So many more.* As a diehard reader, there's nothing I dislike more than stupid conflict and misunderstandings that stand in for actual conflict during a story. This became more pronounced during the indie romance boom, as there were not traditional editors and publishers acting as gatekeepers over what writers could and could not put in books. This was both incredible and annoying.

What I have gathered from reading an extraordinary number of romance novels is that some authors have never had a healthy relationship modeled for them, nor have they experienced healthy relationship behaviors. Just because other authors write about dysfunctional relationships and call it romance doesn't mean you should write the same types of relationships or relationship behaviors.

I certainly do not exempt myself or my titles from criticism either. I've written things that were not the best examples of a healthy, functional relationship. After all, I used to live in an unhealthy, dysfunctional relationship. But that's okay. We're all learning as we go.

The healthier and more functional your relationships are in your life, the more likely your characters are going to have healthy and functional relationships in your fiction.

Yes, conflict is the lifeblood of fiction, but it doesn't have to be dysfunctional conflict. This is probably why a lot of the conflict in my books tends to be externally oriented. I don't like to write heroes and heroines who have so many personal problems that the entire relationship in the book is spent learning how to treat each other in an acceptable manner. Other people can write those books. I prefer to write books that transport readers into an alternate reality, where heroes are heroes and heroines are heroines and they don't do crappy, shady, underhanded stuff to each other because they have mommy or daddy issues. I prefer healed masculine and feminine energy in both my hero and heroine so that they are capable of loving each other so deeply and beautifully that their love has the power to move readers to tears and inspire them to love just as deeply in their own lives.

Dysfunctional relationships and the conflict that stems from them create an altogether different sort of romance than the type I personally prefer to read and write.

If you want your characters to argue and fight about stupid things and have dumb misunderstandings that substitute for real, interesting, page-turning conflict, that is always your choice as the author of the story. However, I would recommend that real conflict is much more intriguing and leads to a better overall reader experience. After all, a lot of readers escape into romance novels because of what they don't get in real life. They don't necessarily want more dysfunctional relationships or disrespectful, cheating, or backstabbing behavior in their fiction too. However, some readers do. Some don't know that there's any other option out there. You can write whatever you want, but I maintain that amazing fiction calls for epic romance.

Relationships aren't easy, in real life or in fiction. They take work to create a great one, whether it's real or not. Your relationship style and personality will undoubtedly filter into your work. Make sure you recognize it so you can ensure you're writing the kind of romance you want to be known for —inspiring and uplifting or something else. It's always up to you.

I love *love*.

I love that love conquers all.

I love that people do things out of love for others that they would never find the courage to do otherwise.

Love is an inexplicable, amazing force of nature.

It's incredible.

When you unleash real love in your romance, magic happens. Hearts are opened. Readers are moved. It's amazing. Don't underestimate the power of a well-written romance and happily ever after, which, of course, starts with amazing characters and requires an amazing relationship to be built within the pages of your story. Don't worry if it sounds daunting. It's not. Just go with the flow and see where it takes you. You can always edit and fix it later. Give it your best, and remember, rewrites are where the magic really happens.

Tropes

A discussion of romance wouldn't be complete without mentioning tropes. I don't think a lot about tropes while I'm plotting or writing, and I'm sure there are some authors who don't even know what they are. So, what are they? Tropes are common types of storylines. In romance, they're really popular with some readers. Readers often hunt for books by trope because they want more of the same, but different.

One of my favorite romance tropes was always a good marriage of convenience. That's when a couple gets married for a reason other than love but then falls in love throughout the story anyway. You can write that trope an infinite number of different ways, and I've written more than one story where it shows up.

Tropes can be timeless, or they can be trendy. There's always a trope that's hot among readers, which means authors who chase trends will often write whatever trope is popular. You can see this clearly every time the *secret baby* trope comes back around and there's a massive glut of this type of story in the market. Other tropes are love triangles, second-chance romance, forced close proximity, enemies-to-lovers, workplace romance, and more. There are *tons.* You can look up lists of popular romance tropes and spend time digging through more obscure ones as well.

Tropes can be really fun to write because there's a basic expectation on the part of the reader about what's going to happen. It can be an easy way to throw yourself into the storyline and use your creativity to make it uniquely your style.

Only you can decide whether you're going to chase trendy tropes or just have fun with whatever organically comes through during your creative process. I don't write for trends. I never have. Writing a book is too much work to try to write and release one in hopes of riding the coattails of a popular trope to bag more book sales. I've always figured that by the time I get the book done, the trend will have already moved on to something new, so I've never bothered to try to keep up with them.

That's turned out to be a really good choice for me. If you're not following trends, then chances are, *you're setting them.*

My best advice, *always*, is to write what you love. Don't be surprised if writing what you love leads to your books being loved by readers. It's a natural progression.

If you want to write all well-loved tropes, go for it. It can be super fun, and you can find tons of success doing it, if that's what you love.

My three *marriage of convenience* stories are three of my bestsellers. I didn't set out to write that particular trope for any of the books, but at the time of writing them, I genuinely loved reading that style of story, so it came through me organically in my own work, and my readers loved it.

Readers love tropes. Again, it goes back to them wanting the same story, but different. If you love to write tropes, write them. Follow your fun. This world is your oyster, and tropes can give you tons of inspiration to write amazing fiction.

FOURTEEN
LANDING THE PLANE

In order to finish a book, you have to make the book important. Finishing a book requires single-minded focus that can take over your mind and your life. The energy that it takes to finish a book is *real*. It's like those last pushes from a woman giving birth. You have to *want to finish this sucker so much*. It can be a very joyful experience, but the energy that it takes to finish the process is *raw*. You have to gather all of your mental, emotional, psychological, and creative resources to get this project across the finish line.

You have to *land the plane*. You have to get this sucker down from the heights of conflict that you've pushed it to and figure out a way to resolve everything, satisfy the reader, and make it through those last scenes to the most beautiful words in the world to a writer—*The End*.

It's a lot. I'm not going to lie to you. To finish a book takes all the energy that it took to start the book and *so much more*. Landing the plane is no joke. It will draw on all your reserves and force you to focus so much energy into one place that you can blow the roof off a house. It's wild.

You are the conductor of the symphony, bringing the orchestra to an amazing crescendo and holding the audience in spellbinding awe while you weave the story together, tie up threads, wrap up conflicts, put subplots to bed, and do creative acrobatic tap dancing to make everything you've spent an entire book building come together, make sense, and reveal all your twists and whodunits with perfect timing and absolute maximum emotional impact.

This is a beautiful part of the book. This is also a part of the story where your mind can start freaking out because it honestly has no idea how to pull this stuff off. Your mind can't solve all these potential plot problems and plot holes you need to wrap up so you can mark this baby off as *done*. That's why self-doubt creeps up so often at this point in the creative process. Your mind isn't equipped to solve all these problems by itself. If you think you're doing this alone and *you* have to come up with all the solutions yourself, it's a daunting prospect. But when you know you aren't doing this by yourself and creative flow is right there with you, coming up with amazing solutions that are so freaking brilliant that you could *never* have thought of them yourself … it gets a lot easier.

First, remember our rule from earlier: No panicking. Do not panic. Ever. It helps nothing. It solves nothing.

Second, tell any negative voices in your mind that *they are wrong* and they have no place in your life.

Then, start thinking about how awesome it is that you're about to finish a book. Start thinking about how cool it is that there is a perfect solution for everything that's going on in the story, which will pull it together and make you look like a creative genius who planned all of this. You didn't, but it doesn't matter. What matters is that no problem is too difficult for creative flow to solve. What matters is that no matter what corners you might have written yourself into, creative flow can help you find a way out of them and make it all work.

I can't tell you I know exactly how this works or what the steps are in this process. Every single book is different. What I do know is this: if you build your story one interesting, riveting scene at a time—inching up your tension and throwing exciting stuff at your characters when necessary, taking them to the brink of despair, where it looks like all hope has been lost to allow for their personal transformation —then *you are on the downhill slope, and this book is almost done and about to be amazing*!

All that's left is the resolution of the major conflicts, which you will do with maximum emotional impact and kick butt delivery and timing—which you have to be excited about and feel your way through—and then you have a scene or two after the conflict is resolved to give the reader a *ton* of good-feeling moments, where they can bask in the joy of the characters' happily ever after or other triumph. Then, for the greatest levels of reader satisfaction, you come up with an epic epilogue, and, *bam*, your amazing fictional work is *done*. That's literally what it takes to land the plane.

I understand this discussion doesn't write the end of your book and finish it for you, but it sums up exactly how I approach and think about the entire process.

Endings have to be incredible. It's a rule of amazing

fiction. But don't worry about it. Actively, do not worry. If you know you need an amazing ending, all you have to do is put that intention out in your thoughts and start thinking about it. You know the drill already: stay open and receptive and then pay attention. Gold and magic will come to you. The answers exist. There's always a fabulous solution, even to your knottiest plot problem. I promise you this. You can always fix the book, and you can always land the plane. It's the toughest part of the journey, but you can totally do it. It's an adventure. You don't have to know what's going to happen for it to turn out really, really awesome. All you have to do is have some faith in the process and think about the story, the characters, the conflict, the subplots, and all your loose ends. How can you resolve all these pieces in the most memorable, entertaining, and exciting way that will give the reader complete and utter satisfaction? That's the route I take to write amazing fiction.

Also, remember all those breadcrumbs, threads, and random stuff I suggested throwing out along the way? Now is the time to grab on to any of those lifelines that you need in order to make this story altogether awesome. And always remember, even if the ending of your first draft doesn't feel amazing the first time you write it, that's okay! Everything is fixable in rewrites. I have seen absolute magic happen and okay stories turn into epic ones.

You are a creative genius. *Of course you can make this epic*. If you believe it and you keep your mind open for solutions, scenes, and anything that can help you, the Universe will send help to you. Don't forget, you might need to enlist the assistance of others who have access to a different set of options in creative flow. Don't feel stupid. Talk it out with a safe and trusted plotting partner or sounding board. If that isn't possible, then spend some time with yourself, preferably in or near water or in nature. There is magic available in the water of your bathtub or shower, just like there is in nature. Still your mind. Chill out. Let your mind clear or wander.

I'll *never forget* thinking I'd really gotten myself into a dead end at the end of my first trilogy when I had *absolutely* no idea how to wrap it up. I had three books almost done, and I didn't know how to land the plane. So, I took a bath. While I was lying in that bathtub in my rental house in Midland, Michigan, a wild and crazy idea came to me that not only provided a shocking end to the story, but also laid the groundwork for an 11-book series and lots of fun crossover character interactions in other stories. It turned out to be super fun for me and for my readers.

Bottom line: There's always a solution. Keep an open mind. Put in the time, effort, and focus necessary. You will land the plane. You will finish the book. It's only a matter of time and creativity.

PART THREE
THE REST OF THE PROCESS

FIFTEEN
THE MAGIC OF REWRITES

Rewrites are not my favorite. I don't think they're anyone's favorite, but I could be wrong. I honestly often find them painful. Sometimes painful in the extreme, if I draft the manuscript exceptionally quickly and I'm under a tight deadline. But whether they are painful or joyful, the magic happens in rewrites.

Yes, there are authors who write one draft of a book and call it good. Some of those authors even have shelves of *New York Times* bestsellers. As I mentioned before, one thing you learn quickly as an author is that just because a book sells a lot of copies, it doesn't mean it's a great book.

So, how do you put out a *great book*? How do you write *amazing fiction*? The best way I know how includes intensive, sometimes-grueling rewrites.

I rewrite nearly every single sentence in my entire manuscript when I'm doing rewrites. I don't start with a fresh, empty document or anything like that, but I do touch every single sentence. I fix everything. Even things that other people think are perfectly fine and should be left alone.

I'm a ruthless rewriting maniac.

But here's the trick: when I'm doing rewrites, I'm not doing them alone. I'm *never* doing any of this creative stuff alone. It's me and creative flow. Never underestimate the power of that invisible force of nature to completely transform your story from okay to incredible.

In order to do that, however, you have to be willing to do the work. Creative flow will help you every single step of the way, but you have to be there—fingers on the keyboard, attention totally and completely focused, your mind enmeshed in the story, and the outside world completely forgotten.

You cannot do rewrites that will produce magic without your total attention, complete dedication, and single-minded focus.

It's not always the most fun part of the process. For me, it's freaking hard sometimes. It's intense. I work for hours straight, completely losing track of time and only coming back to the "real world" because I'm starving, I need the bathroom, I'm exhausted, or creative flow has decided I need a break and the spell has been broken.

For the last book I published, which wasn't fiction, I was treated to the joy of feeling creative flow right there with me, helping me revise every sentence I had written. Instead of painful, these rewrites were actually fun. I didn't just do one round of them either. Over the course of about two weeks, I rewrote the book four or five times. Obviously, each time I went through it, I touched less. But I was *ruthless*. I also read it out loud every single time. Anything that makes me stumble while reading is fixed. Anything questionable that I don't know easily and intuitively how to deal with in the moment is highlighted to discuss with Jake later to get another opinion. That particular rewriting process was harder than writing the book even though it was fun. But the book would never have been as good as it turned out without the rewrites.

It's the same for all of my fiction books. Rewrites are an inescapable part of the process. If you read a book that's good, but not great, there's a decent chance that the author skipped intensive rewrites. I get why they do it—because who wants to reread and rewrite the whole dang book, especially after just finishing it? Pretty much *no one*. It's a part of the process I honestly wish I could skip, but I never do. Intentional, focused rewrites elevate your book beyond a lot of other creative work out there that wasn't rewritten with such care and commitment.

If you want to write amazing fiction, you have to be willing to go above and beyond and do things other authors will not do. This takes dedication, effort, and relentless commitment to producing the best work you possibly can. That's what separates the good from the great.

The first chapter will always be the hardest to rewrite, in my opinion. At least, it always has been in my experience. You're just getting into rewrites, and you're questioning everything. You've hopefully come to terms with the fact that you have a lot of work ahead of you, and you're willing to do whatever it takes to make this story the best damn story it has the ability to become.

Make sure you have a quiet space, where you can work completely uninterrupted. I'm talking about shutting out the entire world. You have to. As you get going, the goal is to become totally immersed in the story and forget everything else about the world and your entire life—just like the reader wants to do. When you sink into that connection, with total focus on the story, creative flow tends to take over. The rewrites and edits you make aren't really coming *from you*. They're coming *through you*. Sometimes, it feels like they're coming out of seemingly nowhere. Things that might not have bothered you before are suddenly fixed in ways that you perhaps didn't expect. It's a really magical process, but you have to be committed to slogging through the hard work until it turns into magic.

Rewrites are the most intense part of my writing process. Without them, my books would not be amazing. That's the truth.

I remember one story that I just couldn't get to come together with the same style and awesomeness that my books were known for. That wasn't acceptable to me. I recall sitting in bed one night, laptop on my lap, Jake sleeping beside me, unwilling to quit until the book was amazing. In the darkness, something took hold of me, and I saw the solution to my issue. I had to make the readers think one thing and then spring the truth on them somewhere else. It was the only way to save the story and make it interesting, memorable, and hopefully, if I could pull it off, epic. The pressure of the task was intense because this was the follow-up to my first major best-selling trilogy. Hindsight has shown me that the pressure I put on myself was also absolutely stupid—a mistake I learned not to make again.

But somehow, someway, out of my sheer determination

and refusal to quit until it was amazing, the story came together. It was in the wee hours of the morning when I finally felt it click. I knew I had done it—but definitely not all by myself. Creative flow and I had managed to fix the trilogy that I'd thought might end up in the garbage. Talk about a huge relief.

Never underestimate the power of creative flow. I repeat this because it's important. If you believe in your story and you're willing to do anything within your integrity to make it the best possible story it can be, including doing all the hard work that no one really wants to do, I firmly believe you will get there.

Your intention matters more than the circumstances. If you don't give up and you keep believing in yourself and your story, creative flow can help you get where you need to go.

It might not come as a voice in your head, like it often does for me, because everyone is different. But it could come through the voice of your trusted writing confidant, through a book you read because you just needed a mental break, through some random idea that seemed to pop into your head out of nowhere, or some other way. It's always there, somewhere, willing and able to help you. You just have to be open to the myriad of different ways that help can materialize.

But above all, if you want to write amazing fiction, *don't skip rewrites*. Give them your time and your energy. The effort will elevate your work to new heights. Skipping them means that you didn't do everything in your power to write the best book you possibly could.

Even with all my insanely short deadlines, including that

time I wrote my first *New York Times* best-selling trilogy in six weeks, I have never skipped rewrites. Never. Not once.

That's where the magic happens, and I aim to deliver magic to my readers *every single time.*

Pro tip: Knowing when to take a break in rewrites is just as important as doing them. When you're exhausted, fatigued, your eyes are crossing, and it feels like everything you're reading is garbage, *take a break.* Save your document, step away from your computer, and allow yourself to rest and recharge before you take a sledgehammer to your book and destroy it. Rewrites require the precision of a scalpel. Not a sledgehammer or flamethrower. The value of taking a break during rewrites at the right time cannot be overstated. You're not trying to destroy your masterpiece. You're simply making it the best it can possibly be.

Know when to hold them and know when to fold them. Then, go back to your work, refreshed, recharged, and ready to rock. Whatever seemed like a pile of crap when you were tired, crabby, and overworked will feel much more palatable to work with and improve when you're feeling rested and at your best. Your state of being matters a *ton* while you're doing rewrites. Take care of yourself and listen to your body. Give yourself what you need to make it through an intense and often-grueling stage of the creative process. Be kind to yourself and those around you while you're in the midst of rewrites. It will serve you much better than the alternative.

Never forget, the goal of rewrites is magic. Not destruction. Don't worry; you can do it. I believe in you.

The Gift and Art of Receiving Feedback

I was told by a developmental editor many times that feedback is a gift. While I firmly believe that is true, you have to be careful whose feedback you invite, what you do with it, and how you let it affect you.

Someone who takes the time to read your work, thoughtfully consider it, and give you feedback is a person you will most likely want to thank heartily. People have lots of other things they can do with their free time that do not include helping you. Always be grateful for someone who is willing to give you their time and their insight. It is a gift.

However, not all feedback is created equally. Sometimes, you're going to get feedback that you completely disagree with. Remember, *this is your story*. First, check yourself to make sure you're not getting caught up in ego. That's really easy to do when someone is giving you constructive criticism on your baby, whether it's a beta reader, a critique partner, an editor, or someone else. After all, that's what your creative work is—your baby. Regardless of how detached you might feel—or not—it's something you are birthing that no one else can birth. Of course, it will feel scary to get feedback at first. It's scary for everyone, not just you. But ultimately, you have to face that fear if you want to share your work with the world. It's just one more step in the creative process. Learning how to deal with feedback so that you can use it to improve your work rather than destroy your creative confidence is another key part of the process.

I sent the first chapter of my fantasy story to a few people, and I was minorly freaking out when I didn't hear anything for days. The first place my mind wanted to go was, *Is it so terrible that they don't want to tell me what they really think?* Old me would've kept running down that road, but wiser me let it go in favor of assuming that not everything was about me and these particular people, who weren't seasoned beta readers, might not have had time to read it yet.

Rule number one with feedback: Don't start jumping to conclusions before you've even heard anything. It doesn't do you any good. Don't assume *anything.*

When I did get feedback, it was along the lines of, *It's awesome. When can I read more?*

Wouldn't I have felt silly, thinking the chapter was terrible when my early readers were just trying to keep up with their own lives and didn't realize that I was a vulnerable creative in the early stages of creation, waiting on pins and needles, to get a reaction to my work?

People don't think like that unless they are another vulnerable creative being who has been in the very same position, waiting on feedback. It's hard to understand if you've never personally experienced it or if you don't work with creative artists regularly. We are a different breed.

While the validating feedback I got was awesome, that's not the kind of feedback we necessarily need to learn how to deal with to improve our work.

The question becomes, *What would I have done if they'd come back and said what I created sucked or wasn't good or needed major changes?*

First, consider who the feedback is coming from. Is this person someone who has all sorts of experience with assisting in writing amazing fiction? Has this person written amazing fiction? Does this person know way more than you about storytelling? Does this person have a ton of experience with giving useful and valuable feedback on written work? If yes, take the feedback seriously and sit with it. Don't be surprised if, initially, you want to tell them how wrong they are and never speak to them again. You honestly might feel like that, but try to keep it under control. That's your ego talking. Your ego only wants feedback that says, *It's amazing! You're amazing. Everything you wrote is amazing. You did everything right!*

And while that is certainly gratifying and validating feedback to receive, it isn't the most helpful if you're trying to up your game and make your book the best book it can possibly be. Generally, you want *something* you can work on. But your ego doesn't want that. Getting feedback that says you mucked up a chapter or the story seems to be going in a weird direction that doesn't feel right anymore or the hero is acting in a way that no reader will believe *sucks*. It does hurt to get feedback saying you didn't do a great job, no matter who it comes from. But it's okay. Because without that feedback, you wouldn't know what someone really thought when they read the book. Without that feedback, you'd find out about the parts of your book that sucked when you read your reviews instead. *That sucks even worse.* And it's way harder to fix.

Take the hard feedback early, while you can still easily fix the story even if it's a lot of work. Regardless of who the feedback is coming from, try to look at the book objectively and determine whether the change is in the best interest of the story. Will it genuinely make the story better? Is there some part of you that thinks the feedback might be accurate and the person giving the feedback is right?

It will always be tempting to say, *Well, that's just one person's opinion, and I don't feel like doing all that work to change it, so I'm just going to let it ride and hope for the best.*

I don't care who the feedback comes from—an expert or an amateur. I can't do that. I have to sit with the feedback and really think about it. *Is my ego getting involved? Do I just not want to do the work because of all the effort and energy it will take?* I go with my gut.

Often, I get a sick feeling in my stomach that tells me I can't go forward in my process until I address whatever it is that caused someone to get hung up. As I stated earlier, I'm in this for *the best possible story I am capable of writing.* I'm in this for *amazing fiction.* I'm not in it for "letting it ride and hoping for the best." That's a great way to invite crappy reviews that are based on facts, which other people might agree with when they read the story too.

It probably shouldn't be too surprising, but I know authors who do this. I also know authors who read their reviews after release and see something and say, "I knew that would come up."

Well, crap, Nancy. If you had known there was a chance something would come up in a review, why the heck didn't you fix it in the book when you had the chance? Like *before* you published it?

Yes, it's sometimes painful, writing a book. Yes, sometimes, you just want that sucker finished so you can move on with your life and never think about these plot issues or these characters ever again. Sometimes, like I mentioned before, you might just want to put your characters in a car and blow it up with a car bomb—like a very successful author friend of mine really wanted to do with nearly every book she wrote—just so you can write those magical words *The End* and be done with the whole thing.

That's normal. That's all part of the creative process.

But you only get one chance to make a first impression with your book. Make it the best damn first impression you can possibly make. If you know there's an issue that has come up with your beta readers, critique partner, developmental editor, copy editor, or someone else who has read the book before it is published, *address the issue so there's no longer an issue that might come up in your reviews.*

I heard another author once say something along the lines of, "If there's a lamp in your book, make sure you put a lampshade on it."

Little things can pull a reader out of the story. You don't want that. That means they might put the book down. You want them riveted by the story—totally lost in the world of your creation. You want them hooked from page one until they hit *The End*. If you don't fix the little issues that come up in your feedback, then you run the risk of breaking the magic spell you've spent so much time and effort to weave for your readers.

Why would you do that?

I wouldn't do that.

I fix every single thing I possibly can. I don't care how sick of the book I am. How much I don't want to work on it anymore. How much I just want to be *done* with the story. I still fix it. I am still 100% committed to delivering the best work I possibly can to my readers in exchange for their hard-earned money. "Good enough" is never good enough for me.

I keep going until it is *the best story* I can possibly write regardless of what it takes or how long it takes. That's a major key to writing amazing fiction. Go above and beyond what anyone else is willing to do, and you will create work that's unlike anyone else's. It's a fact.

However, you will receive some feedback that does not necessarily merit changes. In his book *On Writing*, Stephen King talks about keeping score when receiving feedback. If three people think something should change and one person doesn't, he changes it—even if he's the one person. However, he also talks about the fact that you, as the author, are always the tiebreaker. If it's two versus two, go with what you feel is right.

This means, you have to learn to trust your gut. You have to learn to trust *yourself*. If you don't trust yourself, you will be tossed about on the waves of constructive criticism. I don't know how I know what is best for the story. All I know is that I have to feel my way through it. If someone offers me an idea or a new angle or some kind of feedback, I pay very close attention to my initial reaction.

If it makes me feel sick or it's sickening for me to read or hear the feedback, I step away and take a breather. For whatever reason, I'm too close to be able to process it, but I never forget that initial reaction.

Oftentimes, a developmental editor or editor would add a comment to a book about something that had to be changed to suit them, and I would *vehemently disagree*. First, I would take a deep breath and check my ego. *Is it because I don't want to do the work or because I don't agree with the person?*

If my disagreement is truly vehement and I see the issue completely differently and I think they're just straight-up wrong or misinformed, then I don't change it. I'm not in the business of people-pleasing when it comes to developmental editors and editors. They're human too. They do not always know what is right for my story, and they might not always know what's right for yours.

You have to be strong. By staying committed to what's in the best interest of the story, I sidestep my ego most of the time. Instead, I think about what's truly the right move to create the best experience I can possibly give my readers. It might not be what the reader thinks is the best, but they're not writing the book. I can only do *my best*. No one else's.

Treat feedback with care. Be grateful for it. It's awesome to get. Sometimes, you learn things that can save you so much grief down the road because you just didn't see it from the perspective of someone who was *not* writing the book. But in the end, every decision you make in this story is up to you. You are the final say. It is your name on the cover. It is your reputation at stake. If your editor thinks the book will be terrible unless you do X and you think X would ruin the story or change it in a way that you do not want it to be changed, then trust yourself. Editors think like editors. Authors think like authors. But only you can think like you and create the magic only you can create.

Take what resonates with you, leave the rest, and get back to work.

SIXTEEN
EDITING AND PREPARING TO PUBLISH

If you want to be traditionally published by a publishing house, some of this stuff won't apply to you, but I'm including it anyway because it's valuable information that can help lead to success. The first thing I must share is the truth: self-publishing is not for everyone.

Self-publishing is for those who want to and are capable of running and managing their own self-publishing business in addition to writing the books. You have to do more of the work yourself, but you get to make the final call on everything. Your word is law. No one tells you what to do. No one tells you what you can or cannot write. Plus, you don't share your royalties, like traditionally published authors do. Instead of royalties of the typical net 35% of the sales price of the book, you get to keep anywhere from 60% to 70% of the sales price or more. Doing the extra work is lucrative, but only if you can handle it. If you want to be successful at this, you cannot only be an author—you must also be a CEO. You must think like a creative being *and* a business person. Granted, you probably should if you're a traditionally published author too. After all, this is your business, your income, and your profession, if you do it well. If you are a type-A personality, self-publishing just might be for you. To determine if this is the correct path for you, I highly suggest reading *The Naked Truth about Self-Publishing* to help you decide. Massive thanks to Jasinda Wilder, a wildly successful *New York Times* best-selling romance author, for being kind enough to recommend it to a random fan who was writing her first book. It contained life-changing advice that led me to extraordinary success.

I know nothing at present about being traditionally published. I've never done it. I have, however, sold over five million books in 16 languages as a self-published author, and I haven't even been published for a decade yet.

If you're on the fence about which direction to go, read *The Naked Truth about Self-Publishing* and talk to other authors who have been traditionally published. Most don't say, "Yes! I absolutely love being solely traditionally published," and I've been around hundreds of them. Some, however, do love solely being traditionally published. It all depends on the person and the experience they've had. Plenty of authors love publishing in a hybrid fashion—having some books published traditionally or by an Amazon imprint while also maintaining a self-publishing business of their own. One #1 *New York Times* best-selling author described this model to me as like writing some books for wholesale but with a guaranteed paycheck and writing some books for retail with a potentially bigger upside. I can see how publishing in this hybrid fashion would appeal to some authors, but I was always interested in maximizing my return on my books, which meant that I wasn't willing to sell the rights and potentially give up a huge upside. When you knock a self-published book out of the park, it is *magical*. Money practically rains from the sky. It's freaking awesome.

As you can tell, I'm very fond of being a self-published author for many reasons. I have had opportunities to be published traditionally by major publishing houses, but no one has ever shown me conclusively that they could do something for me that I couldn't do for myself. When that day comes, I'll hear them out and perhaps have a different answer. But for the time being, I adore being a self-published author because of the sheer amount of freedom and opportunity it affords me. Only you can decide what's right for you in your particular circumstances.

Now, let's dive into the rest of the process from the point of view of a self-published author.

Edits and Editors

I've had two editors—almost three—in my fiction career.

My first editor would send me back pages and pages of the book with no changes on them. I would send her back all of my edits after her edits and ask her to review them to see if I was correct about additional changes that needed to be made. I have a fairly good grasp of grammar due to my high school senior English teacher—thank you, Mrs. Stoffan, for teaching us to diagram sentences and for not giving up on us. If you do not have a good grasp of grammar, it's going to be hard to know if your editor sucks or if things are being missed that shouldn't have been missed.

I've read *many* an edited book with errors, both from big indie authors and from massive publishing houses. I used to delight in finding errors in books for some weird reason. I think it meant they were human, too, and I felt like a genius for catching them. I doubt I'm alone in that.

But reading books that are poorly edited is a terrible reading experience for a reader. Especially for the kind of reader who reads a lot of books. They might not know what makes a book well edited, but they know a poorly edited book when they see one. It's like what the United States Supreme Court said about pornography—you know it when you see it.

If you are not confident about grammar, find someone who is to read your edited book to see if your editor sucks, if you have such a suspicion. I once had a very successful *New York Times* best-selling author ask me to critique and line-edit an edited book so she could prove her suspicion about how poorly her editor had edited. She was right in that instance. My point is, it's not unusual to find bad editors. Finding good editors is important, and finding a great one who meshes with you and your writing style is even more important.

My second editor and I parted ways after over 30 books together due to a variety of reasons, including the most important one—she was ready to retire from editing.

That editing relationship was a massive part of my life for eight years. I was writing up to nine or 10 books per year. My life rose and fell based on my editing deadlines and where she could fit me in, or move something when I was behind or struggling, or when I decided I wanted to write a trilogy instead of a stand-alone. I was not the easiest client to accommodate because I go where creative flow takes me regardless of the amount of work it takes or how different the result is from my original idea. I'll do whatever is in the best interest of the story, whatever it takes.

Make sure you and your editor, if he or she is going to be a significant presence in your life, have a functional, honest, transparent, respectful relationship. It's really important. Your editor is an integral part of your team, not just someone who provides a service for you. If you're going to go to the trouble and effort of writing amazing fiction, don't varnish a masterpiece with Rust-Oleum. Get a great editor. The best you can afford. Make sure they are not manipulative or have weird emotional or control issues. If possible, find someone who is healthy, has few health problems, and doesn't have a dozen children who are always sick. Your deadlines are important. Your publishing schedule is important. Find someone who won't constantly let you down, but instead goes above and beyond to help you out. In return, always pay on time and be a great client. Thank them in your acknowledgments sincerely. Recommend them to other writers. Be flexible when they need you to be, so long as it works both ways. It's an important relationship, so you need to find the right person. Also, recognize that it might take a few tries to find the right person. It's always a good idea to read the acknowledgments of books you love and keep track of who edited them. If you see a name pop up constantly, contact that person and see if they're taking clients. If they are, let them know you're interested and you would love to do a couple of pages of test editing to see if you might be a good fit.

If you don't do a test edit on a few pages, occasionally, you might have someone edit an entire book in a style that you do not like or that crushes you emotionally. Once upon a time, I didn't take my own advice and trusted that because multiple successful *New York Times* best-selling authors highly recommended an editor, that meant that specific editor would do a great job for me that I loved too. Instead, I opened the edited file, read a chapter, cried, closed the file, paid the editor her money, and never opened the file again. I had to pay to have the entire book reedited by someone else. Was that the best way to handle the situation? Doubtful, but I couldn't change my release date because I had a preorder locked in and I couldn't handle wading through what had happened to my book during edits. We just weren't a good fit. What I'd expected was not what I received. You can avoid that whole situation by asking for a test edit. If the editor won't test-edit a few pages for you, then he or she might not be the right person for you.

At the time of writing this, I'm also in the market for a new editor. So, I'll have more experience on this subject soon. First, however, I'm going to write the book without worrying about an editing deadline. It might not be the smartest move because great editors can book out for months—or years—in advance, just like other super in-demand service providers. Others might have closed client lists. Others might only take seasoned authors and not want to "train" newbies. But I'm taking a leap of faith on this one because I don't need an editing deadline to push me to finish the book. While that was extremely important during my early days, it's ultimately not the healthiest way for me to work anymore. Only you will be able to tell what is best for you. I have 41 published books under my belt, so I know myself and my creative process extremely well. I make decisions that are right for me regardless of what standard wisdom might advise. Hopefully, by the time I'm ready, I'll have found the perfect editor for the project.

I'm hopeful because it's also really important to remember that there are a lot of editors out in the world who need clients, especially clients like me, who write amazing fiction, do intensive rewrites, deliver clean manuscripts, and make an editor's job as easy as possible for them. If someone can fit you in on short notice, it could be a red flag—just like the contractor who can get to your construction job right away when the rest are booked for the year. But there are plenty of exceptions to most rules.

Use your gut. Get a test edit. If someone bleeds all over your page—edits the heck out of it and it's all red from track changes—don't curl up and die immediately.

My second editor's work looked like a war zone after my first editor, who had a very light hand. I ended up *loving* her heavy-handed edits for my fiction. She was *very* thorough. It also allowed me to get lazy in my writing and increase my speed. I got lazy in my sentence structure, and she would fix it. Perhaps that's not the best outcome from having an awesome editor, but it's a bad habit that can be broken.

When you're writing that many great books in one year,

something always has to give. Thankfully, I had assembled a great team who I could lean on—sometimes *heavily*—to meet my ambitious goals of publishing many memorable, amazing, beloved five-star stories. Consistently. Sometimes up to nine times per year! It was a lot. I drew on the energy of everyone around me—from my husband, my author friends, my beta readers, my assistants, my developmental editor, my editor, my proofreaders, my readers, and more. Something that intense takes a lot of support. I was a freight train. No one could stop me. I was determined to deliver every time, over and over. Faster and faster. You can't do that without a great editor.

Also, a warning from the burnout queen: you can't do that forever either. Eventually, the piper must be paid.

But a great editor can make your life *much easier*. Find out how many passes the editor does—how many times they read the book—and find out if they do an audio round of edits. This can be huge in delivering a cleaner manuscript back to you. My editor wasn't happy if I found more than five errors or things she had missed during her work. They should all fit on one hand, was her theory. I agreed. We both had high standards. An audio round of edits—where the editor listens carefully to the book and picks up on anything that doesn't sound right—is an awesome thing for you, the client. My proofreader would always say that I delivered the cleanest books she'd ever proofed. My editor and I both considered that a huge compliment.

Pay editors what they're worth or what they ask. If they are terribly underpriced, tell them they should charge more. Most won't or will only raise their prices very little. It's easy to get priced out of the market, but someone who is great should come with a matching price tag. If they're super cheap, there's a chance you're getting what you pay for. Developmental editors are all over the board on cost. If you need one, only you can decide what that's worth to you.

I was writing excellent books very quickly. My creative well wasn't enough to support that alone. It took three people's creativity and ideas to make a lot of my books happen, plus creative flow, because they were written so rapidly. Again, this is why it's easy for me not to have an ego about stories—most of mine wouldn't have been nearly so good if I had been concerned about using only my ideas. It doesn't matter to me. I do whatever is in the best interest of the story. Does it bother me when some of my readers' favorite moments weren't my idea? Not at all. I think it's funny. I'm the workhorse of the story. I'm the one committed to bringing it to life. I have the initial concepts and characters. I assemble the team. I ask for the help. I am the conductor of the orchestra. None of it would happen without me. The readers don't care. They just want a memorable, amazing experience. That's what they're paying for.

Bottom line: Get a great editor. Don't allow yourself to be bullied by anyone though. Be committed to what's best for the story and be determined to see that through until the very end.

Also, if you're publishing traditionally, whether with a big or small publishing house, know that you likely won't get to pick your editor, and there's also a chance your editor might be able to force you to make changes to your book that you do not agree with, if you signed a contract giving the publisher that level of authority over your work. I have never gone down this road, so the only editing relationships I can speak on are those of the self-publishing variety, where I, as the author, have the final say. I don't know if I could create my brand of amazing fiction any other way. I've never been sufficiently enticed by a traditional publisher to give it a try. Only you can decide what is best for you with regard to your particular circumstances, opportunities, and process. Choose wisely.

Editing with Narration in Mind

When I do my rewrites—also referred to as self-edits—I read the manuscript aloud. Every word of it. I read it out loud because I want to hear how it sounds.

Is it easy to read? Is there a good flow? Where do you stumble? What sentences are smooth? Is it going to sound good in audio?

Anything that doesn't pass my rigorous scrutiny is fixed.

Then, when I get edits back from my editor, I read the entire book out loud without the changes showing. I don't like to get my ego involved with edits. I don't care if my editor's way sounds better than my way. I just want the book to sound the best it possibly can. As I read my edits, I highlight anything that makes me stumble or that I don't like. Sometimes, I'll be reading and think, *What the heck did my editor do to this part?* And then later, when I'm looking at the document with the changes showing, I'll realize the answer is *absolutely nothing.* The part I didn't like was something for which I was wholly responsible. Reading the manuscript and simply highlighting what I don't like—and adding a comment about it and a fix that might immediately occur to me—allows me to read the book with the edits and catch both the things that my editor changed that I don't like and things my editor didn't change that I don't like. In the end, it doesn't matter. I just want the book to be the best it can possibly be. It's not an ego contest. It's always about what is in the best interest of the book.

By editing this way, my audiobooks tend to be better than average and get great reviews. However, that is also obviously due in huge part to having great narrators. An awesome audiobook is much more likely to happen if you write great stories and then hire wonderful and consistent voice actors who deliver fabulous performances. But I still try to make the job as easy as I can by reading my manuscripts aloud to help me catch things that I might not have otherwise caught.

Proofreading

If you want your book to have the least amount of errors possible, then try my old law-school trick: read it backward, sentence by sentence. You won't get caught up in the story and miss things, the way you would if you read it from the beginning. If I'm super-duper committed and I have time, this is my last pass through the book in my writing process—after a professional editor and a professional proofreader have already worked their magic. It's time consuming, but you'll find things everyone else missed.

And, yes, I do believe you need a professional proofreader. It's important. Even editors who do three passes and an audio round can miss things. I used to use three proofreaders, but then I realized one of them was the best of the three, so I decided to trust her alone with my work. I was never disappointed. She found errors that *everyone else*, including me, missed. It was really quite impressive sometimes.

Find someone with eagle eyes. Not just someone who says they are good, or claims to be good, or who just likes to read and knows some grammar stuff. Find someone who is a legitimately good proofreader. It's a skill. A good one is a godsend. I'm so thankful for mine, and I will be super bummed when she retires because she has been so reliable and awesome.

As you can tell, I believe proofreading is important and should be a valued part of your process. A reader deserves a well-proofed book. Every error is a chance to pull the reader out of the story. Every time they have to think about whether you messed up is a moment they aren't thinking about how amazing the story is. Take the time. Make the investment. Try to deliver the most perfect creation possible to your readers. They deserve it. They work hard for their money, and they are choosing to spend it on something you created and are contributing to you living your dream. The least you can do is get your book proofed by someone who does it well.

If you don't know if your proofreader is good, you will likely find out in your reviews. Mostly, you'll read, *Poorly edited*, or, *Was this book edited?* Like I said before, readers might not know what's wrong with the book, but they'll know something's wrong. Don't give them any reason to do anything but enjoy the crap out of your story, so much so that they want to experience it over and over again. Good proofreading is a part of that.

Make sure you do at least one pass yourself, if at all possible. I've broken this rule before out of necessity and sanity, but I highly recommend always proofreading it yourself at least one more time.

Formatting

Good formatting is important in both print and e-book. A book should not be hard for your readers to read. That would deliver a poor reading experience, which ultimately doesn't work out in your favor. Thankfully, good formatting doesn't have to be elaborate at all. It can be very basic, and that's great. As a matter of fact, I do not like ornate formatting unless it's in a fancy edition of a hardcover book.

If you sell a lot of e-books, I also recommend against super-fancy formatting. You don't want the formatting to take away from the reading. Make it easy to read. Make it simple. The more ornate the formatting is, the more you run the risk of distracting your readers from the story *and* being charged higher delivery fees to get your e-book to your readers due to large file sizes.

Vellum is a formatting program that my team uses that has simplified the formatting process across our extensive catalog. It's easy to use, and we can be nimble when changes need to be made, especially to back matter, as opposed to waiting on a freelance formatter to make the changes. With as many books as we have in our back catalog, that ability to react quickly matters to us.

However, if you want beautiful formatting on special editions, you can never outdo a visual artist. Find books that you love the way they look and check the copyright page or the acknowledgments to see if the author discloses who designed the interior. If they did, reach out to the person to see if they will design a book for you too. The worst they can say is no, so it's worth an email at least.

Covers

Great covers sell books. That's not in dispute. But you can't rely on a great cover to create amazing fiction. What's inside the book has to be just as good or even better than the most incredible cover. If someone buys a book because of the cover, that's awesome! Woohoo! You just snagged a new reader! Keeping a new reader is harder, however. Whether or not they buy another book of yours depends entirely on whether you did your job between the covers. If you did, then covers aren't nearly as important.

It's really easy to fall into the trap of believing that your cover is what sells your book. I don't believe that's necessarily true. Yes, readers love fantastic covers, and that's even truer depending on the genre. But don't believe your cover is the only reason someone buys the book. It's not. The cover doesn't give them those thrills or emotionally satisfying moments or the happily ever after they might be craving.

Don't get so hung up on covers that you forget what's really important—the book itself.

You can spend all sorts of money on covers. And after you write your amazing fiction, you should absolutely invest whatever makes sense to you and your budget on the best cover you can.

Do you need a custom photo shoot to get a great cover? Absolutely not. This might sound funny, coming from someone married to a gorgeous cover model, but I'm committed to being honest. From personal experience, aside from shoots where my husband was the model, I can tell you that custom photo shoots often end in disappointment because of the resulting photos they yield. You might have the perfect idea in mind for your photo shoot to nail that fabulous cover you can see in your head, but it's not unusual to get something back from the photographer that is vastly different than what you were expecting and hoping. When you shell out a serious chunk of change for the shoot, those results can be devastating. Granted, it can also go the exact opposite way, and you might be thrilled with the most beautiful images that bring your vision to life. You just never know exactly what you're going to get with a custom photo shoot.

You can also hire a great designer who can take stock photos and turn them into something so unique that no one will ever know it was a stock photo to begin with. It's generally a lot more affordable and a lot less stressful. However, the most important thing is to have a cover that shows off your book to its best advantage. Look at other covers in your chosen genre. What do you like about them? What do you dislike? What is selling? Which ones make you want to pick up a particular title?

At the end of the day, as a self-published author, you decide on your own cover. That can be thrilling, or it can be daunting. Either way, I highly suggest you ask a few people you trust to take a look at your cover as it's coming along to get feedback. Often, you'll be surprised how others can easily pinpoint something that's not working on your design or something that needs to change when you couldn't figure out what it was. Another suggestion I've heard is to take your mocked-up cover—or a proof copy of your book—to a bookstore and actually show it to real perfect-stranger readers wandering the aisles of your genre and ask them if they'd buy a book with that cover. I haven't actually done this, but I know at least one *New York Times* best-selling author who swears by it.

By way of confession, I have to admit that I don't really enjoy the cover creation process. It has been that way for me since my first book. I generally leave them for dead last in the publishing process, after the book is done, but other authors will have a cover made before they even start writing the book. In the self-publishing world, you decide. If you love covers, then you'll have a blast with them. Enjoy it!

To me, it's so much easier to write the book than to worry about the cover. I deal with the cover when I have to. I also bring in help. I don't do this stuff on my own. While my design eye has gotten a lot better over the years out of necessity, I'm like a lot of people—I know what I like when I see it, and I know when I see something I don't like. But I don't always know how to express my thoughts in a useful fashion, and often, I don't know how to fix the design to get to what I do want. Thankfully, everything has always worked out fabulously because I have no problem asking for help.

If you don't have a particularly good grasp of graphic design, don't worry. You can absolutely still end up with amazing, jaw-dropping covers. You do, however, have to approach the process as a *process* and not be upset when a designer sends you something that looks like crap or is a million years away from your vision. It's okay. That's just a jumping-off point to get to where you want to go. Don't settle until you have a cover that you or the people around you, whose help you are leaning on, really love. I've come so close to settling so many times, but because the people around me insisted I ask for at least one or two more changes from the designer, I ended up with covers that were so much better than what I would've settled for. Don't settle. But also, don't be surprised if you have to pay extra for a million rounds of changes. A designer's time is valuable. Make sure you compensate them fairly. Try to make every interaction you have with a service provider a win-win situation. Don't be the jerk client who is terrible to work with and argues over every invoice.

Also, don't be surprised if cover designers aren't always the most professional and timely people with whom you work. They are artists too. I don't know if this is everyone's experience, but it took me *years* to find someone I meshed with well, who did amazing work, was punctual and professional, and always delivered what I needed before I needed it. Contrast that to a designer who doesn't even give you the first draft of the cover until the day before you need the final version. I've lived that scenario too. Even though the cover ended up amazing, it wasn't worth the stress I'd had to go through to get it. I never did that again.

Only you will be able to decide what kind of cover you want and who you want to create it. There are tons of talented cover designers in the world with all sorts of different price points and budgets. Choose what works for you. Feel your way through it. Be willing to try different designers, especially if you're treated poorly by one.

I don't care how many *New York Times* best-selling covers a designer has created. It doesn't give them a right to treat you poorly.

Reputations are gained and lost constantly out in the world. I have a whole list of cover designers I will never recommend to anyone and some I will actively recommend *against* using if I'm discussing the subject in conversation. The list I will recommend is extremely short. I have high standards. I expect professionalism, originality, creativity, top-notch work, and excellent client service. If a cover designer, or any service provider, can't deliver those, I move on.

My time and my work are valuable. I treat them as such. I highly recommend you do as well. Mostly because if you accept crappy treatment, you are *allowing* that person to treat you in a manner that is inconsistent with how you believe you should be treated. After making that mistake for many years, I learned that people only treat you poorly because you allow it. When you stop allowing it, things change. Yes, you might lose the relationship, professional or personal, but you gain self-respect, and that is priceless.

Even if you're a nobody—and everyone but celebrity authors start out as a nobody in the publishing world—you should still expect professional and courteous treatment. Anyone who treats you like crap because you don't have a title in front of your name will always treat you like crap, even after you have a title in front of your name. At least, that has been my personal experience. Some people are just like that. Move on and find someone you actually enjoy working with and paying for great work. There are tons of amazing designers out there, and one or more of them will be absolutely perfect for you.

SEVENTEEN
LETTING GO OF YOUR CREATION AND OFFERING IT TO THE WORLD

Letting go of your creation and offering it to the world can be hard for people. But at some point, you have to stop editing and proofing and tweaking, let go of your creation, and send it out into the world for other people to enjoy. This is actually the point of being an author. Write the book, then release it.

Why is that hard sometimes?

I'm sure there are a million reasons, with each author having their own flavor, but I think a lot of it has to do with fear. The moment you release your book, you are letting it go. Letting it *fly.* You're stepping away from it because everything that happens after release truly has nothing to do with you. The book has become its own entity. It's something that can stand on its own two feet and live on without any more of your editing or effort. Obviously, this is only true if you write the absolute best book that you can, rewrite the crap out of it, have it edited professionally, review those edits in minute detail, have it proofread—possibly more than once— and then proofread it again yourself. Once you've ticked all those boxes and the book is as amazing and as perfect as you can humanly make it, it's not your business anymore. You release it, market it, and collect the royalties.

How the world reacts to your book is also none of your business.

You did your part. You created something that hadn't existed before, and you worked *hard* on that. Well freaking done! What readers do with it after is really not up to you. All you can do is your very best. If your best isn't good enough for someone, then oh well. That reader isn't for you. Your book will not be for everyone—trust me on this. Don't worry about writing something everyone will love. That's a surefire way to write a tepid, *meh* book. Some people might hate what you created. That's okay. It's not for them. It's for the people who love it. For the people who will reread it a dozen times and feel like they're reconnecting with old friends. *Those are your people*. At least, those are my people.

Do the work. All of it. Write. Rewrite. Edit. Proof. Proof. Format. Release. If you've done everything you can do, then there's truly nothing left to worry about.

Let it go. Let it fly. Let it become the property of readers all over the world, who will claim it as their very own favorite. After all, that's what happens when you release amazing fiction.

Reading Reviews

Let's make one thing clear: Reviews aren't for authors. They're for other readers. Keeping this in mind makes it much easier to ignore them. Yes, you can spend lots of time reading reviews, especially bad ones, and put yourself in a negative state of being that damages your creativity. I don't recommend it. It's also a great way to ruin your day and your mindset.

If someone doesn't like your book, then it wasn't for them. That's okay. Remember that not everyone is supposed to like your book. It's okay if they don't. As I mentioned before, writing a book to please everyone in the world is a great way to write an okay, very middle-of-the-road book. Five-star books aren't written to please everyone. Amazing fiction isn't written to please everyone. Please yourself first and then hopefully at least some of your beta readers. They don't all even have to like it for it to be an incredible book.

I've written plenty of books that the people who beta read for me don't like that much. Some of those have become my most successful titles commercially and financially. In fact, my most successful trilogy is likely one of my most hated stories by many readers. It's okay. It's not for everyone. I'm not for everyone. It's taken years for me to be at peace with that, but the quicker you can get there, the more awesome your life will be every single day.

However, I am not saying I don't read *any* of my reviews at all. I read a few of the early ones, from readers of advanced review copies, purely to see if I did what I'd set out to do. I learned this from a more successful author. She taught me that if you read a few of the early reviews—and, yes, my team handpicks those for me these days—and you see that the people who usually love your books also loved this one, then why bother with reading any further? It's a habit I've adopted, and it has worked well for me.

I don't hate myself. That's why I don't read my Goodreads reviews. If you do want to hate yourself and question why you ever wrote a book to begin with, you can get to that place pretty quickly by reading reviews on Goodreads.

If there's something to be learned from the reviews, have someone else read them for you. I had a developmental editor who would read all the bad reviews on my books during release week. I didn't ask her to do this. I don't know why she even did it, but she would pull out a few useful nuggets to apply to future books on occasion. I, however, never went down that rabbit hole. I always know that I have things I can improve in books. I try to make every book better than the last in some way. Continuous improvement never stops.

However, one author I know actually found a great beta reader because she broke all the rules and reached out to someone who had written a review, picking apart one of her books. I believe they worked together and maybe even improved her writing in future books. That's awesome, but it's not for everyone.

If you do go down the road of reading your reviews, be kind to yourself. The goal is not self-flagellation. Keep your head up. Just by writing and publishing a book, you've joined a pretty elite group of humans. Not everyone can finish a book. It's hard. Then, there are *tons* of people with stacks of completed manuscripts in their drawers or in files on computers that they've never had the courage to publish. Remember how brave you are. Remember how much courage it takes to walk this path. And then give yourself some grace. You're learning. You're evolving. You're improving. Your first book won't be the best book you ever write. Hopefully, it's just the best book you could write in that moment, under those circumstances, with those skills and that knowledge. Keep learning. Keep trying. Keep adjusting. You'll get better, and so will your reviews.

Writing the Best Book You Can Will Always Be the Best Marketing You Can Do

Marketing is part of being an author. However, the best marketing you'll ever do is writing the best book you possibly can. Writing books that sell themselves will save you a lot of time on the back end. After all, you only have to write the book once. You want to sell the thing forever. Write a great book once, over and over again, and you'll find a lot more success down the road. Even more than writing the best book you possibly can, consistently writing and publishing amazing books is exceptionally good marketing.

If you are an automatic "one-click author" for readers, then those readers won't think about buying your books. Your books have become a must in their life. They might even follow you in some way or check on your website on a semi-regular basis to find out when your next book is coming. They'll be really disappointed—but often understanding—when you take a break from writing. These people are your super fans. They give you their hard-earned money every single time you release a book. That is a gift. It's amazing. You are one of their *favorite authors*. It still blows my mind to think that there are people out in the world who think of me in the same way I think of my favorite authors. They think things like, *Wow, I'm so glad she decided to write books. I hope she keeps doing it forever.* It's mind-blowing and a huge honor.

That kind of trust from a reader is important. You are a go-to author. There is no second thought about anything when it comes to reading your work. It doesn't matter where the money has to come from; that reader will be reading your book as soon as they possibly can after release.

That's a big deal. That's a huge deal, really. I do not take reader trust lightly. Ever. And if you want to have a successful fiction career, I believe you should care about reader trust too.

Readers trust you to deliver a book that will live up to their general expectations about you as an author. It doesn't matter that every book isn't their favorite—we all like some stories more than others, even from our favorite authors. But readers who trust you will always appreciate a well-written and well-thought-out story with your brand of storytelling and style, along with great editing, that's well proofread and neatly formatted. That's the deal. That's the social compact. Readers give you their money, and they expect something in return. You have to live up to your end of the bargain every single time or else that reader trust is damaged.

Is it up to you how readers react to your chosen plot and characters? No. Not at all. You'll probably never know how they reacted. But even if they don't like the story, if it's well done, they're still going to buy the next book you write.

When don't readers buy the next book? I can only tell you what I do as a reader, and that's what I use as a rule of thumb as an author. If an author I love and buy without hesitation every single time totally botches a book, I give them grace. Everyone has stuff that doesn't come together quite right. Or perhaps they were writing too fast or crazy stuff was happening in their personal life and their focus wasn't there, but the deadline was. It happens. I give everyone a second chance, if they've already earned my trust.

What happens though if the author needs *another* second chance? If an author botches two books in a row, I'm left wondering, *What happened to them?* My trust in that author is now damaged. As a reader, I now have to think about whether or not I'm willing to buy a third potentially botched book. That hesitation means this formerly *automatic one-click* author has become a *hmm, I wonder if this book will be good or not* type of author.

I've experienced this over and over and over as a reader. I've had authors who never let me down for years suddenly lose the plot and publish books that I couldn't finish, no matter how hard I tried. It happens. Sometimes, that just means it's time for you to move on to someone new.

But I've never wanted to be that kind of author for a reader. I want to be the *must-buy-every-single-time author because she always delivers her best and her best is always pretty damn good, whether or not I love every single part of the book.*

I wanted to write books that readers didn't just buy and read once. I wanted to write books that readers read over and over again, going back to them like old friends and favorite movies. Why? Because that's what I did as a reader. I'm a rereader through and through. I appreciate well-written characters and beautiful storylines that make you believe anything is possible and that love always conquers all. Because it does. That's why people are drawn to happily ever afters in all formats of entertainment. It's the completion of the hero's journey. It's the journey of each of our souls. We all face challenges and overcome them, often transforming us into new versions of ourselves. That's why we like to read and watch people do it better than us, in more exciting circumstances—and with wittier dialogue. The characters rise to the occasion, say things we aren't brave enough to say and do things we aren't yet brave enough to do. At least ... not until we are inspired by hearing someone or seeing someone or reading about someone doing something truly heroic. We change throughout the course of our lives, and we love to watch characters change and grow and succeed in overcoming their demons, whether internal or external. We love to see people experiencing their dreams coming true.

Art imitates life. So, give people good stories, well told, well written, with memorable characters that feel like old friends when they come back to the book over and over again. Make sure your book is free of errors and plot holes. Keep readers in the story. Drag them through every single page, keeping the tension rising higher and higher as you build. Put true stakes on the line. Give it some tension. Challenge those characters. Let life take them where it will. See how they react —because react they will. Let creative flow give you direction. Follow it. This is how amazing fiction comes to life.

And if you get bored with your story, take a break until you're ready to figure out how to fix it.

Some of the best writing advice I've ever heard came from crazy-successful *New York Times* best-selling author Abbi Glines. She said, "Stop where you're bored and go back to the last time you weren't bored and start over from there."

It was simple but invaluable advice. If you're bored with your story, there's a chance that readers will be bored too. And if readers are bored, they might not finish the book. And if they don't finish the book, they might not buy the next one. See where I'm going here? Success requires consistently good books.

All you can do is your best. But do that. Over and over and over again. You'll get there eventually, if you're determined enough. And then who knows what could happen in your life as your amazing books take off to the moon and you have a writing career you couldn't even imagine was possible? That's what can happen when you write amazing fiction.

My Second-Best Marketing Tip

When you finish that book you absolutely love, *talk that baby up!* Tell your audience why you're proud of it and why you're excited for them to experience it. Tell people why they need to read it. Use your genuine excitement and enthusiasm to sell your book. *Always be real*. People can spot a fake easily and tell if you're just putting on a show.

After writing an amazing book, this is the best marketing you can do. It will serve you well with every book.

But you have to write awesome books you love in order to be able to do it. If you can't muster genuine enthusiasm for the book you're selling, then reassess what you wrote. If you don't love it, why should anyone else give it a shot?

The easiest way to sell something is to sell something you believe in and that you believe your audience needs.

There are lots of choices of books to buy and read out there, so why should readers plunk down their hard-earned money for yours?

Be YOU. Be unique. Be a fresh voice in a crowded sea. Write stories only you can write. Do it *your way*. Take chances. Be memorable. Write for *you*.

Writing incredible books is your *job* as an author.

Fancy marketing tricks can totally get a lot of people to read a less than incredible book. It happens *all the time*. But your goal isn't to sell a lot of people one book if you're trying to grow a career as an author. Your goal is to grow your *automatic one-click* reader base. Like we talked about before, those are the people who adore your books so much that they don't care about the title, the cover, or the synopsis. They just care that you wrote another book. Those are the readers who show up time and time again.

You can't buy that kind of reader loyalty, and you can't create it with fancy marketing tricks. You have to earn that trust with every single book you write. You earn it with consistency and by continuing to write amazing book after amazing book.

But make sure you do it at a pace that doesn't burn you out, that allows you to continue to refill your creative well, and that doesn't place undue stress on your body, mind, or soul. That's easier said than done, but it is possible.

And if you feel like no one is paying attention to the brand-new book baby you just released into the world, that's okay. They probably aren't. It's totally fine. This isn't a *get rich quick* scheme. Writing amazing fiction is way too much freaking work to be one.

Don't worry about an amazing book you wrote that isn't selling. Go back to work and write another amazing book. I know it sounds like a lot of work, but that's generally the right choice. Why? Because that amazing book you wrote that isn't selling is just a check waiting to be cashed. When your time comes and one of your books breaks out, it's highly likely that many of your new readers will go back and read all of your previously published work. Writing an amazing book is *always* worth it. However, sometimes, you do have to have the patience to allow readers to find you first. Can you imagine how much bigger your breakout success would be if you hit the jackpot on book 10 rather than book one? It's an exponential deluge of awesome because you don't just have one book to sell—you have 10. I only point this out because it happened to me on book three, and I've seen it happen to others. Financially, breaking out on book three was a much bigger windfall than if I'd broken out on book one. Kristen Ashley, a wildly successful, beloved romance author with a cult following, had *dozens* of books published when the world caught on to her unique brand of awesome. Can you imagine how amazing that must have been for her?

I know we're all programmed to want everything to happen immediately, but there are definite advantages to divine timing.

Write the best books you can. Shout about them from the rooftops. Tell everyone why they're awesome. Then, go write another great book. You never know which one will be the magic to take you into a life beyond your wildest dreams.

EIGHTEEN
FINAL WORDS FROM A CREATIVE REBEL

Learn the Rules—Then Break Them

There are a lot of rules about writing fiction. As I mentioned earlier, I suggest acquainting yourself with them, learning why they exist, and then breaking whichever ones you want to break. But if you never learn the rules, there might be ones that you break in ways that shouldn't be broken, which will end up pissing off readers and not help your career.

If you are not a reader of your genre, then you might find it valuable to learn about what readers of your genre like and don't like. Learn why they like what they like. Try not to do the things they absolutely hate and will not forgive. They might never buy another one of your books again otherwise. Do your research. Learn about your genre and potential readers. Learn about writing craft. Then, you can decide which rules you want to follow.

There are also tons of rules about grammar and syntax. We were all taught in school that we're not supposed to start sentences with *but* or *because*. But I do it all the time. I did it right there. Because I wanted to. Because I can. Because I'm an author. I can make up words. I can take creative license. I can break rules. But I try to do it with purpose, for impact, and to write the best stories I possibly can.

Learn the rules—as many of them as makes sense for you. Then, be a rebel and break whichever ones you want.

It Only Takes One Book to Change Everything

In January 2015, I sold 101 books total on Amazon for the month. By mid-February, I was selling 100 books *per hour*.

What changed?

I released a book, and it went *wild.*

I'd had no expectations for the book. In fact, I was *sure* that my first trilogy coming later in the year would be *the one.* My breakout release.

I was wrong. I'm wrong about these things a lot. I *never* know which book is going to be the one that goes crazy and sells a bajillion copies. I also never know *when* it's going to happen. That's the beauty and magic of this gig.

It only takes one release to change everything. And it doesn't even take that. It only takes one moment, one sale, one *something*, and it feels like your entire life changes overnight.

When you hear those stories of overnight success 10 years in the making, it feels a lot like that.

Suddenly, you're *it*, and what you created is on everyone's lips.

But the danger is getting caught up with hoping every single book will be the one. If it's not, that's a great way to set yourself up for disappointment, and disappointment is not the energy you want around you.

A better idea is to do the best work you can do—every single time—and just keep going. It doesn't matter which book takes off. When you believe it's just a matter of time and you keep going and keep writing and keep believing, it can happen for you. You likely will not be able to predict it. I have *rarely ever* been able to predict my own success. I'm nearly always wrong, it seems.

You have to let go of wondering how long it will take and just get back to work. It doesn't matter how many "flops" you release. Every single book you put out is simply a check waiting to be cashed when you do break out. If you break out on book one, that's awesome. But also, people will only have *one book* to buy. And by the time you finish your next book, they might have already forgotten about you and moved on.

When I didn't break out on book one, or book two, I just told myself that my flops were simply checks waiting to be cashed, as good as money in the bank someday. And I was right. It happened.

It only takes one book to change everything. Believe it can happen for you, and it can.

What Does It Actually Feel Like to Write with Creative Flow?

It's hard to describe what it feels like to write with creative flow because writing with creative flow consists of those moments when you're fully immersed in the present, in the now. You're not thinking about anything. *You* aren't even really there. At least, you have no sense of yourself. It's like you don't exist, except as a transmitter and transducer for the magic that is flowing through you. It's like *I* cease to exist and become completely submerged in the creative process. It's not *me* doing anything. I'm just part of the magic that is happening—a necessary part of the process, but not separate from the process.

It sounds absolutely insane. But it feels like coming home. You're not separate anymore. You are a part of life, and it's flowing through you to express itself in ways that haven't been expressed before.

Time ceases to exist.

Everything around you fades away.

Noise and sound disappear.

It's just you and the words flowing through you, typing as fast as you can to keep up with the magic.

It's just you, living completely in the moment, doing what you're meant to do. It's unity between you and creativity. Alchemy takes place as the energy flows through your body, transforming invisible ideas into an incredible story that you gift to the world.

It's magic.

That's the only real description I have for it.

It's invigorating, energizing, and yet demanding and exhausting. Your mind and body become a channel for words and wisdom you cannot see, but you can feel.

You can't force it. You can't demand it. You can only create the conditions whereby it can happen.

It's amazing.

Instead of you figuring out what to write, say, or type, it's like you slip into a jet stream, a trade wind, or a current, and it lifts you up, takes you along, and pours through you so that words come effortlessly and without a single thought from you. You're simply along for the ride, acting as the channel and the scribe for the magnificence that comes through.

It's a wild experience. It's also a very normal, everyday experience. That flow state is available anytime, if the conditions are right. You can tap into it when doing tons of different things. Writing is just one example.

You see it with athletes all the time. It's when their movements and motions become effortless. When they merge completely with the game in the present moment and it becomes absolutely beautiful.

You stop thinking and simply be and do. When you're in flow, you're being moved by the rhythm and stream of life itself. It multiplies what you could do by yourself, making it effortless and incredible.

I've never written a single book by myself. Creative flow has been right there with me every time. Maybe it doesn't take over for every word or every scene, but every single time, when I sit down to draft, I allow myself to be consumed by the flow. There's no telling where the flow begins and where I end. In those moments, I don't even exist. I am nothing but awareness and keystrokes.

It's epic. It feels amazing. The work it produces is awesome, if you're brave enough to run with it without hesitation or question.

If there's one place that makes writing amazing fiction as easy as possible, it's right there, in the creative flow.

Trust yourself. Believe in yourself. Prepare yourself. Embrace the beauty of silence. Eliminate all distractions and interruptions. Create the necessary conditions. Then, get to work and see where it takes you. Disappear into the magic. Reemerge into your body when it releases you. Be amazed at how awesome you feel afterward about what you've written.

That, my friends, is a creative rebel's guide to writing amazing fiction.

RECOMMENDED READS

Meg's Must-Reads for Writing Amazing Fiction
GMC: Goal, Motivation, & Conflict by Debra Dixon
Techniques of the Selling Writer by Dwight V. Swain

Meg's Suggested Reads for Writing Amazing Fiction
On Writing by Stephen King
Write Your Novel from the Middle by James Scott Bell
How to Write Dazzling Dialogue by James Scott Bell
Super Structure by James Scott Bell
Scene & Structure by Jack M. Bickham

Meg's Suggested Read for Writing Romance
Passionate Ink by Angela Knight

Meg's Must-Reads for Creative Longevity
Deep Work by Cal Newport
Rest by Alex Soojung-Kim Pang
Play by Stuart Brown

Meg's Must-Read for Indie Publishing

The Naked Truth about Self-Publishing by The Indie Voice

THINGS NO ONE TOLD ME

- You can write whatever you want, no matter what other people might think about it. You don't need anyone else's permission to do it either. You can just decide to do it and then do it.
- Sometimes, when you think you're procrastinating, you're learning. Intelligent and strategic procrastination can be very helpful and align you with perfect timing.
- If you wait around to write *only* when inspiration strikes, you might never finish a book.
- Deciding you're going to do the damn thing for real is one of the most important decisions you could ever make.
- There are infinite possibilities for every choice you make in writing a book—and in life. Sometimes, it doesn't matter what you pick. Sometimes, you just have to *pick something* and keep moving. Don't

worry about making the wrong choice. Just go forward.

- Don't worry so much about the words you put on the page, especially in your first draft. It's all fixable. Remember, "You can't edit a blank page." —Nora Roberts

- You will probably not like all your books the same. But remember, every book you write will be someone's favorite even if it's not yours.

- At some point, you might think you've peaked in your art. Keep going.

- Selling books depends a lot more on your attitude, self-belief, and commitment to excellence than marketing.

- You will face challenges. Whether or not you succeed depends on you and your attitude and how you feel about yourself and life.

- No one else has to believe in you for you to be successful. Only you have to believe in you. It literally doesn't matter if no one else believes you can do it as long as you believe you can do it. Prove the doubters wrong.

- Seven questions determine success for me: (1) How bad do you want it? (2) How hard are you willing to work for it? (3) How much do you believe in yourself and what you are capable of? (4) How much do you enjoy what you're doing? (5) How positive is your attitude and self-talk? (6) How good are you at visualizing yourself as successful? (7) How strong is your faith in yourself and in life?

- Your motivation matters. Make sure yours is solid and not ego-based.

- It takes an insane amount of self-belief and courage to be successful as an author. Don't worry; you can do it too. Get brave. Believe in yourself. You're more than halfway there.

- You are most powerful in the present moment. Don't waste it, being distracted. Get off social media. Don't scroll your life away. Write amazing books instead.

- If you chase money at the expense of everything else, you very likely will end up miserable. Focus on the reason you need the money, not the money itself.

- Don't be afraid to make mistakes, even big ones. That's how we learn. The bigger the mistake, the bigger the lesson. It's not a mistake if you learn from it; it's a learning experience.

- There is no one way to be successful as an author. Everyone does it differently. Find the things that work for you and stick with them. It doesn't matter if no one else does what you do.

- Sometimes, the Universe will ask you to prove how badly you want the things you say you want. There will be challenges along the way. You can handle them. You can handle *anything* life brings to your door. *Anything*.

- You can work hard. It won't kill you. But make sure you take care of yourself so you don't burn out.
- The best book you can write at any given moment might not be the best book you've ever written. That's okay. All you can do is your best *today*, and that's all you need to do.
- You have your own unique creative process. Learn about it. Improve it. Streamline it. The better and more efficient your process is, the less painful it is to write amazing fiction.
- Fall in love with your process. It makes everything easier.
- Every step of your career is a testing ground and a learning process. Everything is an experiment. Learn from every result you get, whether it's a triumph or a flop.
- Continuous improvement is key.
- Slow and steady growth is more reliable than astronomical growth—but I'll take both.
- You are not a one-hit wonder. You are a work in process, and you are still getting better.
- Success is like driving a car. You have two pedals —brake and gas. The brake is worry, fear, doubt, comparison, envy, jealousy, greed, et cetera. The gas is knowing what you want, believing in yourself, believing what you want is possible for you, being grateful, having fun, being excited about what you're doing, your positive attitude, et cetera. How fast you get to success depends on

how you drive and which pedal you're flooring. If you keep slamming on the brakes, you're going to get there a hell of a lot slower, and it's going to be a jerky ride. Painful even. If you *never* hit the gas, if you never know what you're aiming at or never believe it's possible for you, you're never going to get there. Most people hit the brakes every single day, whether they're conscious of it or not. They doubt themselves, wondering why it hasn't happened yet, wishing they could be someone else who is already successful. Every single one of those thoughts slows down the journey. Even if they know what they want and believe they can get there, most people constantly sabotage themselves. If you put your foot down hard on that gas pedal and floor this car—knowing what you want, believing you can get there, picturing it in your mind, and feeling good about it—you are going to put yourself so far ahead of the pack that you'll be on a completely different level soon. It all depends on *you*. No one else can consistently and reliably make it happen for you. Only *you*. So, how do you want to drive on this incredible life journey? Only you can decide.

- Your imagination is one of the most valuable and powerful tools you have in your arsenal. Use it!
- Dreams transform into reality when you're in the trenches, doing the work, grinding it out alone, and no one is watching because they're out, having fun. This is where discipline means the difference

between success and failure. This is where the magic happens.

- People might call you selfish for chasing your dreams. It might piss them off. Don't let it stop you. A lot of them have never seriously chased a dream and have no idea how hard it is and how much sacrifice is involved. Don't listen to them. Keep going.

- It doesn't get easier. You get better, more resolute, less apologetic about giving yourself what you need to thrive, and more confident that sacrifices now means success later.

- No one will put your dream first but you.

- Authors don't always want to write, but they do it anyway because the book doesn't get done unless they sit down and write.

- Some of the best words I've ever written and the best scenes came on days when I wasn't really feeling it. I just sat down and did my job, and then magic happened.

- Sometimes, all you can do is show up. Keep showing up. It matters.

UNSOLICITED ADVICE

- Believe in yourself. First. Last. Always. It matters so much more than you might realize.
- Follow your heart. It doesn't matter which book you think will make the most money. Listen to your heart. Write the book that tugs at your heart.
- If you want to be successful, act like you're not only an author, but also a CEO, running a business. You are not just someone with a hobby. If you want a serious career, take it seriously. Treat it with respect. Act like it's a big freaking deal.
- Stay humble.
- Prepare for success.
- Remember, every book is a new chance to break out or level up.
- Money and bestseller titles aren't going to make you happy long term if you're not already happy.
- Enjoy the journey, not just highlights and the paydays. If you only love the end product and hate

the journey, you're going to spend a lot of time feeling self-induced misery.

- Trust that the timing will be perfect. You are not too late. You did not miss out. There is still time for you.
- If you're going to be lazy, be strategically lazy. Procrastinate intelligently.
- Self-doubt will cripple you if you let it. Don't let it. Don't think about it. Just do it. It doesn't matter what other people think or what happens if you fail. Just *do the damn thing.*
- Whether you believe you can or you can't, you're right. *Believe you can.*
- If your predominant thoughts are always about why you can't succeed, you might as well be building the Great Wall of China between you and success.
- Make a vision board. Look at it all the time.
- Make-believe introduce yourself in your head and out loud as you would want to introduce yourself in real life. For example, "Hi, I'm Meggan, and I'm a rock star of an author."
- Things that will derail your train to success faster than anything: comparison, envy, jealousy, worrying about why it's taking so long, fear, judgment, scrolling endlessly on social media, gossip, greed, getting involved in stupid drama, being ungrateful, feeling entitled, and losing faith in yourself.
- Believe it will happen for you.

- Believe with absolute certainty that your success is a foregone conclusion and that it is only a matter of time.
- Do the work and have as much fun as you possibly can while you're doing it.
- You will never please everyone with one book, so don't try. Please yourself. Write the best book you possibly can that *you* love.
- Care deeply about your story and your characters. If you don't care about your story or your characters, why should anyone else?
- Only publish the best possible book you are capable of writing and creating in that moment. Never settle for anything less.
- Don't take the easy way out. Rewrite what needs to be rewritten. Cut the things that need cutting. Be ruthless about excellence. Work hard.
- If your dreams don't scare you, they're not big enough. If you don't feel a little ridiculous about your goals, they probably aren't big enough either.
- Dedicate yourself to mastery of your craft and self-education. You will get better with every book.
- Don't be a copycat. You're a creative genius. Come up with your own ideas. No one likes a copycat, especially the person being copied.
- You don't have to reinvent the wheel every time, but you do need to put your own spin on everything.
- All great writers learned from other great writers. Learn from them. Emulate them—do not copy.

Develop your own style. Become someone other people emulate on their way to developing their own style.

- Kick the negativity out of your head. Shut out all the negative thoughts, like: *I'm not good enough. It's too late. It's too hard. I'm too young. I'm too old. I can't. I'm scared. I don't deserve it.* Those thoughts are lies. Don't give them any energy.
- Read a lot. It helps.
- Look for the good or the lesson in everything.
- Ask questions and then try to find the answers yourself. Don't be a jerk who wastes other people's time because you aren't willing to do the work yourself and you want it handed to you. *No one owes you anything.*
- Prepare for success but get comfortable with failure.
- Learn from others but find your own voice. You might start out wanting to be the next *someone*, but being the best *you* is way more awesome.
- Stop worrying about what other people think.
- Don't just chase money. It's hollow. Chase happiness. Chase joy. Chase appreciation. Chase gratitude. The little moments matter so much. Don't be too busy and too stressed to enjoy them. Savor them.
- Set a date. It changes a dream into a goal.

TROUBLESHOOTING

If you're stuck on what to write next, these are my tried-and-true methods for getting unstuck. Use whichever calls to you or use them all.

1. Take a break and go for a walk, preferably in nature. The solution can come to you more easily when you're relaxed and receptive.
2. Take a break and go have fun. Stop thinking about your book. The solution can come to you more easily when you're having fun and not worrying about your book.
3. Take a plot nap. Remember that magic can come through easily in the falling-asleep phase. Don't forget to catch it. If you fall asleep, then you probably needed a nap. Good job!
4. Write your question down and do some stream-of-consciousness journaling until you've tapped into creative flow again.

5. Talk it out with a safe, trusted plotting partner or sounding board. Magic can come through anyone.

If none of these ideas work, take a day off. Go do something else. Take two days off if necessary. It'll come. Give it time and be open and receptive to your answers coming to you when you least expect them.

If your book is boring or you've lost interest in the story:

1. Go back to the last scene you were excited about or interested in. Cut all the words after that and drop them into a new document called Saved Lines. (Don't ever delete. Always save, even the work you cut). Rethink the direction of your story. Don't start writing again until you're excited about the direction you're going.
2. Don't be afraid to be "mean" to your characters. Blow things up (or people's lives) or kill someone (or their dreams). You never know what's going to happen after you toss your characters from the frying pan into the fire. They'll be okay, and so will you.

If negativity is taking hold or you're experiencing major self-doubt:

1. Remind yourself that you are amazing. You matter. Your work matters. You can do it.
2. Remind yourself that this is not easy, but it'll be worth it. Investing in yourself is the most

important investment you'll ever make. Investing in your art is investing in yourself.

3. Remind yourself that Rome wasn't built in a day. It takes time to write a book. It takes time to create a backlist. It takes *time.* Be patient. If you can't be patient, learn patience.

4. Remind yourself that you want to do this because it's something you're meant to do. It's part of your life journey. You owe it to yourself to see what happens when you make this dream come true.

5. Remind yourself that you are a freaking badass. You're taking chances. You're taking risks. You're brave! You have courage! That's a *huge freaking deal*!

6. Remind yourself that the only thing between you and a finished book is some crap in your head. Tell your mind that your heart is in charge and you're done listening to all the reasons you can't. Focus firmly on all the reasons you *can.*

7. Remind yourself that negativity has never helped a situation *ever.* It's not going to help this one. Always find the positive or the lesson.

8. Remind yourself that every author has felt paralyzing fear and self-doubt. You're not alone. Welcome to the club! It's normal. It's part of the process. Give yourself grace and keep going. Don't let anything stop you.

9. Give yourself a hug. You deserve it. You got this. You can do it.

If you find yourself comparing your lack of success with someone else's success:

1. Stop yourself and start thinking, *If he or she can do it, I can do it.*
2. Remember that someone else achieving what you want or receiving what you want is simply proof that it is possible for *you.*
3. Remember that someone else succeeding doesn't mean you can't. There's enough success and book sales to go around for everyone.
4. Start clapping and cheering and do a little dance to celebrate someone else's success. The energy of celebrating success is highly magnetic and attractive to the energy of success. It doesn't matter whose success you're celebrating.
5. Be happy for other people, sincerely and genuinely. Learn to love seeing other people win.
6. Remember that it's only a matter of time until you experience success. Keep going. Don't quit until you are experiencing your dreams as your reality.
7. Believe it's possible for you. Believe it's coming and it's only a matter of time. Then, get back to work.

If you feel burned out:

1. Take care of yourself. You are the asset. Treat yourself as though your health and happiness are priceless.

2. Take a break.
3. Get whatever help you need.
4. Give yourself whatever you need.
5. Rest and recover. You will live to write another day.
6. Have fun. Do things you enjoy and that make you feel alive.

If you're afraid of what other people are going to think about what you are writing:

1. Stop thinking about them.
2. Remind yourself that it doesn't matter what anyone else thinks of you or your work.
3. Remember that you are writing for *you*, not for them.
4. Remember that your creative work is a gift to the world regardless of what anyone else thinks.
5. Remember that a lot of people are ignorant and believe stupid things. It's not their fault. Have compassion for them. Don't let your amazing creative work become a casualty of someone else's ignorance and stupidity.
6. Remind yourself that this book is going to be someone's favorite book. You have to finish it, do your best, and do the story justice. You got this!
7. Always choose the solution that's in the best interest of the story, whether it feels safe or not and whether or not you want to do the actual work.

Always choose what is in the best interest of the story.

8. You are here to live your life, not someone else's desires for your life. *Be YOU. Write what you love and what you want to write.* Congratulations! You're now a creative rebel!

ALSO BY MEGHAN MARCH

NONFICTION

A CREATIVE REBEL'S GUIDE SERIES

A Creative Rebel's Guide to Winning the Game of Life

A Creative Rebel's Guide to Writing Amazing Fiction

FICTION

The ANTI-HEROES COLLECTION

MOUNT TRILOGY

Ruthless King

Defiant Queen

Sinful Empire

SAVAGE TRILOGY

Savage Prince

Iron Princess

Rogue Royalty

MAGNOLIA DUET

Creole Kingpin

Madam Temptress

*Redemption (**Coming Soon**)*

White Knight

DON'T MISS OUT!

Visit the following links to sign up for my newsletters and receive exclusive content that I save for my subscribers.

MEGHAN MARCH

CREATIVE REBEL

meghanmarch.com/
subscribe

creativerebel.com/pages/
subscribe

JOIN OUR TRIBE

meghanmarch.com/
community

Want to be the first to know about upcoming sales and new releases?
Follow me on BookBub!

ABOUT THE AUTHOR

Meghan March spent 25 years reading romance novels, eight years practicing law, and the last 10 years writing the best books she possibly could. She's a creative artist, a divine adventurer, a force of nature, a race car driver, a visionary, and a philosopher. She lives to love her real-life hero and soul mate and inspire people around the world to believe in themselves and chase their dreams. She's a hermit and a farmer on the edge of a canyon in the forgotten wilds of the Northwest and wakes up grateful for this blessed life every single day.

Connect with her at:
www.meghanmarch.com

Ingram Content Group UK Ltd.
Milton Keynes UK
UKHW041446040623
422846UK00004B/163